W9-AWL-946

THE ARABIAN
NIGHTS

The Arabian Nights

THE ARABIAN

A PLAY

MARY ZIMMERMAN

NORTHWESTERN UNIVERSITY PRESS
EVANSTON, ILLINOIS

Northwestern University Press
www.nupress.northwestern.edu

Copyright © 2005 by Mary Zimmerman.
Published 2005 by Northwestern University Press. All rights reserved.

Printed in the United States of America

10   9   8   7   6   5   4

ISBN-13: 978-0-8101-2094-5
ISBN-10: 0-8101-2094-1

Based on Powys Mathers's translation, *The Book of the Thousand Nights and One Night*, published by Routledge and Kegan Paul in 1986

page vii: Muqadassi quoted by André Clot in *Harun al-Rashid and the World of a Thousand and One Nights*, translated by John Howe

Front-cover photograph: The Madman (Lawrence E. DiStasi) and Perfect Love (Jane Cho), Lookingglass Theatre Company (copyright © Cyndi Finkle)

Back-cover photograph: Scheherezade (Jenny Bacon) and the clarinetist (David Kersnar), Lookingglass Theatre Company (copyright © Liz Lauren)

Professionals and amateurs are hereby warned that this material, being fully protected under the Copyright Laws of the United States of America and all other countries of the copyright union, is subject to a royalty. All rights, including, but not limited to, professional, amateur, recording, motion picture, recitation, lecturing, public reading, radio and television broadcasting, and the rights of translation into foreign language, are strictly reserved. All inquiries regarding performance rights for this play should be addressed to the author's agent, Bruce Ostler, at Bret Adams Ltd., 448 West Forty-fourth Street, New York, NY 10036.

Library of Congress Cataloging-in-Publication Data

Zimmerman, Mary.
    The Arabian nights : a play / Mary Zimmerman.
        p. cm.
    "Based on Powys Mathers's translation, The book of the thousand nights and one night, published by Routledge and Kegan Paul in 1986."
    ISBN 0-8101-2094-1 (trade paper : alk. paper)
    1. Arabian nights—Drama. I. Mathers, E. Powys (Edward Powys), 1892–1939. II. Title.
    PS3576.I66A73 2004
    812'.54—dc22

                            2004020715

⊚ The paper used in this publication meets the minimum requirements of the American National Standard for Information Sciences—Permanence of Paper for Printed Library Materials, ANSI Z39.48-1992.

For the Lookingglass Theatre Company

Baghdad, in the heart of Islam, is the city of well-being; in it are the talents of which men speak, and elegance and courtesy. Its winds are balmy and its science penetrating. In it are to be found the best of everything and all that is beautiful. From it comes everything worthy of consideration, and every elegance is drawn toward it. All hearts belong to it, and all wars are against it.

—Muqadassi, ninth century

CONTENTS

PHOTOGRAPHS

Frontispiece: *The Arabian Nights*

PRODUCTION HISTORY

The world premiere of *The Arabian Nights* was produced by Look-ingglass Theatre Company, Chicago, and opened on September 22, 1992, at Chicago Filmmakers.

Scheherezade	Jenny Bacon
Jester and others	Mark Brodie
Greengrocer and others	David Catlin
Ishak of Mosul and others	Thomas J. Cox
Madman and others	Lawrence E. DiStasi
Shahryar and Aziz	Christopher Donahue
Butcher and others	Christine Dunford
Sympathy the Learned and others	Laura Eason
Perfect Love and others	Joy Gregory
Boy and others	Doug Hara
Clarinetist and others	David Kersnar
Harun al-Rashid and others	Phil Smith
Dunyazade and others	Heidi Stillman
Abu al-Hasan and others	Andy White
Pastrycook and others	Temple Williams
Slave Girl and others	Meredith Zinner

Allison Reeds and Michael Lapthorn codesigned the production; Kenneth Moore designed the lights; the music was created by *The Arabian Nights* company with Bruce Norris as musical consultant. Anastasia Congdon was the stage manager.

The New York City premiere was produced by the Manhattan Theatre Club on March 1, 1994, at City Center Stage II.

Karen TenEyck designed the set, Tom Broecker designed the costumes, and Brian MacDevitt designed lights. Diane DiVita was the production stage manager.

The Arabian Nights was remounted by Lookingglass Theatre in association with the Actors' Gang, Los Angeles, in fall 1997; the Brooklyn Academy of Music, New York, in fall 1997; and Steppenwolf Studio, Chicago, in fall 1997 with set design by Dan Ostling, costumes by Mara Blumenfeld, and lights by T. J. Gerckens.

The cast changes in the 1997 Lookingglass production included Namaa Potok as Scheherezade, Joey Slotnik as the Greengrocer, Adam Dannheiser and David Schwimmer as Shahryar, Jane Cho as Perfect Love, and Anjali Bhimani as the Slave Girl.

Mary Zimmerman directed all three productions.

A NOTE ON THE STAGING

The play is best suited to a thrust stage with the audience surrounding and looking down on the playing area. The setting is simultaneously the darkened chamber of Shahryar, where he sits listening to Scheherezade, and all of the various locations within the stories themselves. The floor is covered with overlapping carpets. Colorful oil lamps hang above both the stage and the surrounding audience. There are several ornate wooden ottomans that form the deck of a boat, a set of stairs, a privy, or whatever else is needed. Shahryar has his own, more royal ottoman. There is a safe corner of the playing area for instruments and musicians. Although doors and entrances are mentioned in the stories, there should be no doors: they are indicated by the sounds of knocks and bells.

All of the performers remain in full view of the audience throughout the play, sitting or lying on pillows on the periphery of the playing space, rising to join the action as needed, adding a bit of costume as they take on a new role. Entrances and exits are not often indicated in the script; generally a character's first line signals his or her arrival in the scene and the last line signals his or her departure. The action is continuous; scenes and locations overlap and dissolve into one another with no more indication than an actor turning in a new direction or perhaps a slight shift in the light, a new sound, or a bit of music.

Scheherezade moves easily between narrating the stories and taking on small parts in them, and she may also shadow the various other narrators of the stories within stories. Once characters begin to tell their own stories, they address the audience and the peripheral performers directly. The "frame" around the individual's story may dissolve, but the overarching frame of Shahryar listening to Scheherezade and watching the tales unfold should never entirely disappear. Although there is a great deal of narration in the play, it should seldom act as a substitute for action or image. The stories are embodied, "seen" as well as "heard."

The music and sound effects are played live. In the original Lookingglass Theatre production, the music was developed by the cast and played on a variety of instruments including saz, oud, harmonium, zither, recorder, tambourine, udu drum, dumbek, djimbe, tabla, and a wide variety of other percussion instruments (sticks, bells, triangle, finger cymbals). Two or more of the performers might be the principal musicians, skilled on many instruments, but they should also play roles in the stories, and every actor should at one time or another play an instrument.

The original division of roles among sixteen actors is given in the "A Note on the Casting" (see page 141).

THE ARABIAN
NIGHTS

CHARACTERS

Shahryar

Wazir

Scheherezade

Dunyazade

Harun al-Rashid

Jafar

Chief of Keys

Madman

Slave Girl

Perfect Love

Sheikh al-Islam

Fools

Prince of Fools

Jester

Jester's Wife

Pastrycook

Greengrocer

Butcher

Clarinetist

Man in the Dream

Chief of Police

Poor Man

Boy

Girl

Sheikh

Robber

Kurd

Persian

Kadi

Abu al-Hasan

First Sage

Sympathy the Learned

Second Sage

Third Sage

Old Boatman

Mock Khalifah (Aziz)

Masrur

Azizah

Other Woman

Aziz's Mother

Girl in the Garden

Characters of the Confusion

Ishak of Mosul

Sheikh al-Fadl

Women by the River

Additional characters include musicians, servants, police, chorus members, a family, and so on.

ACT I

[*On the stage are rolled-up carpets, piled pillows, and stacked ottomans. Hanging lamps are very low over the floor. Two members of the company enter through the audience with drums, take center stage, and begin to play. The other members of the company enter variously and prepare the stage for the play: they toss pillows into the air or to one another; they arrange the props and ottomans; they unroll the carpets. Some take up instruments and join with the drumming. The hanging lamps are raised. When everyone and everything are in place, the drumming stops, and the lights go out. In the dark we hear the sound of wind rushing over the desert—a sound generated by the company. Someone strikes a set of finger cymbals once, an action that will precede the beginning of each new story.*]

CHORUS:
Once there was a king called Shahryar
Who one night found his wife in the arms of a slave;

The world darkened for him, his soul grew sick,
And he killed them both on the carpets of the bed.

[*A* WOMAN *screams. The lights rise slowly on* SHAHRYAR, *with his hand pressing against the* WOMAN's *mouth. Or perhaps he is using the loosened end of his turban, stuffing her mouth or strangling her with it. The* WAZIR *is kneeling nearby, his face averted. The sound of the wind and her struggle continue under the* CHORUS.]

From then on, every night
He marries, loves, and kills a virgin girl,
And when she dies, anything of him that she might have inside
Also dies. And he will never be betrayed again.

SHAHRYAR:
Friend, trust not at all in women, smile at their promising,
For they lower or they love at the caprice of their parts.
Filled to the mouth with deceit, they lavish a lying love
Even while the very fringe trimming their silks is faithless.
Mild love today tomorrow will give way to madness.
Say not, "If I might love and yet escape the follies of loving,"
But rather, "Only a miracle brings a man safe from love."

CHORUS:
This has gone on for three long years.

WAZIR:
Prince of Time, Shahryar—

SHAHRYAR:
Yes? Whom do you have for me tonight?

4

WAZIR:
No one, my lord.

SHAHRYAR:
What?

WAZIR:
The people are all one cry of horror. Many have fled with their re-
maining daughters. There are no more girls to serve for this assault.

SHAHRYAR:
Have you no daughters, my noble wazir?

WAZIR:
O Prince of Time, commander of the—

SHAHRYAR:
Faithful servant, have you no daughters? Two, I believe. Dunya—,
Dunya—

WAZIR:
Dunyazade is a little child—

SHAHRYAR:
Dunyazade and Scheherezade. Two girls, I've heard, who in the mat-
ters of beauty, charm, brilliance, and perfection are unrivaled, except by each other.

WAZIR:
It is true.

SHAHRYAR:

Bring me Scheherezade tonight, and tomorrow bring her shroud. And don't look so sad. You are about to be the father of a queen, if only for one night.

[*The sound of the wind changes to that of morning songbirds.* SHAHRYAR *continues to mutter his opening poem under his breath. The* WAZIR *turns to his two daughters:* SCHEHEREZADE *reads a book;* DUNYAZADE *is sleeping near her.*]

SCHEHEREZADE:

My father, why do you look so sad? Know, Father, that as the poet says, "You who are sad, oh be comforted; for nothing endures, and just as every joy vanishes away, so also vanishes every sorrow."

WAZIR:

Heart of my heart, I can't delay it any longer: you must marry our king and die. Or else let us leave everything we have and run into the desert.

SCHEHEREZADE:

By Allah! I will marry this king. I am—

SHAHRYAR [*muttering*]:

filled to the mouth with deceit

SCHEHEREZADE [*simultaneously*]:

filled to the mouth with stories, and I have a plan by which I will save the daughters of the Mussulmen. And Dunyazade will help.

WAZIR:

Heart of my heart, my daughter—

SCHEHEREZADE:

Father, this is written in my destiny. Now bring me my wedding clothes, and sing me on my way.

[*As the* CHORUS *sings the following,* SCHEHEREZADE *and* DUNYAZADE *travel to* SHAHRYAR's *palace on a camel led by the* WAZIR. SCHEHEREZADE *studies her book and whispers occasionally to* DUNYAZADE, *who holds a parasol over her. Some* MEN *sing "Allahu Akbar" under the others. Toward the end of the song, the sisters* SCHEHEREZADE *and* DUNYAZADE *arrive at the palace, dismount, and bid farewell to their father, who leads the camel away.*]

CHORUS:

Go and be comforted, Child of the Faithful;
What he has written, that you cannot alter.
Go and be comforted, Child of the Faithful;
What he has not written, that shall never be.

I keep the sweetness of my voice to sing to him,
I keep my fairest verses in his praise.
But my voice is not sweet enough to sing of him,
My verses are too small to hold his praise.

Walk on lighthearted; care not, carry nothing.
Fear not what men do, grieve not at sorrow.
Walk on lighthearted; care not, carry nothing.
Fear not what men may do, leave all to him.

[*The music stops.* SHAHRYAR *pulls* SCHEHEREZADE *to him, unsheathes his curved knife, and holds it to her throat.* DUNYAZADE *begins to cry. The following lines often overlap.*]

SHAHRYAR:
What is that noise?

SCHEHEREZADE:
Only my sister crying, Prince of Time. She has never spent the night alone.

SHAHRYAR:
Stop her. Now!

SCHEHEREZADE:
Dunyazade, don't cry. Allah alone lives forever.

DUNYAZADE:
I know.

SCHEHEREZADE:
Someday, Dunyazade, someday in the morning or the afternoon, or in the night, you will join me. We will be together, again. Don't cry—

DUNYAZADE:
But how will I ever sleep—

SCHEHEREZADE:
Don't cry—

DUNYAZADE:
at night?

SHAHRYAR:
What's she going on about?

SCHEHEREZADE:
Nothing.

DUNYAZADE:
How will I ever sleep without your stories?

SCHEHEREZADE:
Nothing at all.

DUNYAZADE:
I'll never hear your stories again! I'll never hear about Ala al-Din or "The Contest of Generosity" or how the Madman got rid of his wife! I'll never hear the tale of "The Dream" or "The Forgotten Melody" or of Sympathy the Learned.

SHAHRYAR:
What's this?

DUNYAZADE:
Sister, your words are so sweet and gentle, pleasant to the taste.

SCHEHEREZADE:
Have mercy, she's just a little—

DUNYAZADE:
I can't sleep without—

SCHEHEREZADE:
child.

DUNYAZADE:
your stories.

SHAHRYAR [*after a pause*]:
I never sleep.

DUNYAZADE:
O Sister, tell us one of your tales of marvel. Tell it now!

SCHEHEREZADE:
Gladly, and as a duty, if the great and courteous king permits.

[*A long pause.*]

SHAHRYAR:
It is permitted.

[*The knife is still at her throat.*]

SCHEHEREZADE:
Have you heard, O auspicious king, of the great and glorious Harun al-Rashid, khalifah of Baghdad, a most wise and generous ruler—

SHAHRYAR:
Harun al-Rashid? Of course! What do you think?

SCHEHEREZADE:
Yes, well—

SHAHRYAR:
Have I heard of Harun al-Rashid? Is this all you have to say to me?

SCHEHEREZADE:
It is related that one night Harun al-Rashid felt himself weighed down by a heavy depression.

[HARUN AL-RASHID *and* JAFAR, *his wazir, come forward. The finger cymbals chime once.*]

HARUN AL-RASHID:
Brother and Wazir, my heart is heavy.

JAFAR:
O King of Time, all joy and sorrow come from within, but sometimes outside shows may have an influence upon these humors. Have you made trial of any outside shows today?

HARUN AL-RASHID:
I have taken up in my fingers and let fall all the jewels of my treasury; the rubies, the emeralds, and the sapphires, but not one of them lifted my soul to pleasure. I have been to my harem and passed in review the white and the brown, the copper colored and the dark, but none of them lifted my soul to gladness. I went to my stables, but not one of my countless horses could amuse me, and the veil of the world has not lifted.

JAFAR:
What do you say to a visit to the madhouse, my lord?

[SCHEHEREZADE *slowly draws away from* SHAHRYAR, *whose attention is taken by the scene.*]

To my way of thinking, the mad have a more subtle understanding than the sane. They behold differences and affinities which are hidden from common men and are often visited by strange visions.

SCHEHEREZADE AND HARUN AL-RASHID:
As Allah lives,

SCHEHEREZADE:
said Harun al-Rashid,

SCHEHEREZADE AND HARUN AL-RASHID:
Let us go at once.

SCHEHEREZADE:
They left the palace and made their way to the madhouse.

[*They approach the* CHIEF OF KEYS, *who bows. The* MADMAN, *in chains, sits in a corner.*]

CHIEF OF KEYS:
We've had a shortage of fresh lunatics lately, my lord. I attribute the falling off to a general deterioration of intellect in all of Allah's creatures. I am pleased to say that I can show you one madman, although, I confess, he does not seem so very mad to me.

HARUN AL-RASHID [*to the* MADMAN]:
Have you been shut away for madness?

MADMAN:
As Allah lives, I am neither raving mad nor melancholy mad. I am neither an idiot nor a normally stupid person. But my adventures have been so singular that, were they written with a needle in the corner of my eye, still they would serve as a lesson to the circumspect.

HARUN AL-RASHID:
Our ears are open, and you have all our attention.

[*The finger cymbals chime once. As the* MADMAN *speaks, he removes his chains and puts on more formal clothing, aided by his* SHOP AS-SISTANT.]

MADMAN:
I am a merchant and the son of a merchant. Before I was thrown into this place, I had a shop in the market where I sold bracelets and other costly ornaments for women. This story begins when I was only sixteen years old and already had a reputation for seriousness, honesty, and chastity. I never tried to make conversation with my women customers and only spoke the necessary words of purchase and sale; I practiced the precepts of the Book and never lifted my eyes to any daughter of the Faith. Other merchants held me up as an example to their sons, for I already knew how to hold myself above desire, and I understood the proper place of women and the proper place of men. One day, as I sat reading my account book—

[*The sound of a shop doorbell. A timid* SLAVE GIRL *enters.*]

SLAVE GIRL:
Is this the shop of the noble So-and-So?

MADMAN:
It is.

SLAVE GIRL:
And are you he?

MADMAN:
I am.

SLAVE GIRL:
I have something for you.

MADMAN:
Well?

SLAVE GIRL:
It comes from my mistress, and—

MADMAN:
You may approach me, you must know the reputation of my honor.

[*She approaches cautiously and hands him a note.*]

SLAVE GIRL:
It comes from my mistress, and she waits the favor of an answer.

MADMAN [*reading with increasing consternation*]:
"Love has filled my soul with wine and gold . . ." ". . . The black scorpions of your hair . . ." ". . . Come with me to the bath, beloved, and I will . . ." What is this?

SLAVE GIRL:
It's an ode.

MADMAN:
A what?

SLAVE GIRL:
An ode. To you. It's from my mistress.

MADMAN [*angrily*]:
Who is this harlot who writes to me?

SLAVE GIRL:
She waits the favor of an answer.

MADMAN:
How dare this foul woman write to me?

[*He steps forward; ominous music. He tears the note and beats the* SLAVE GIRL.]

Carry this back to her! Carry this back to her, Daughter of a Thousand Shameless Horns! Carry this back to your foul mistress! Carry this back to that pimp's bastard, your mistress!

[*The* SLAVE GIRL *runs away; the bell on the shop door rings. The music stops. The* MEN, *including* SHAHRYAR, *applaud. The* SHOP ASSISTANT *gathers up the torn bits of the note and hides them under a carpet.*]

This happened, my lords, when I was only sixteen years old, and I tell it as an example of my virtue and purity at the time. But not to put Shaaban with Ramadan, I will only say that the months and years passed, and I became a man. I began to think it was time for me to marry a wife in the sight of Allah. And I did marry. As Allah lives, I did so.

[*Extremely sensual music and drumming begin.*]

One afternoon, as I was sitting reading my account book, I heard a commotion in the street. I looked up and saw a remarkable thing.

[*A* WOMAN *veiled from head to foot enters, dancing, with an entourage of* WOMEN *with veiled faces. Although they are dressed modestly, their brief, approaching dance is erotic. They stop at the entrance to the shop. The music ends. The bell of the shop door rings.*]

PERFECT LOVE:
Young man, have you a choice of gold and silver ornaments?

MADMAN:
Yes, mistress, I do.

PERFECT LOVE:
Show me some ankle rings, if you will.

[*She sits and lifts the hem of her skirt a little.*]

Try them for me. What's the matter?

MADMAN [*awestruck*]:
I am sorry, mistress, but surely none of this will ever fit your ankle.

PERFECT LOVE:
Do not trouble about them, young man. I will ask you to show me something else.

[*He turns to go. She touches his arm. She is troubled.*]

Tell me, is it true then, as they say at home, that I have an elephant's legs?

MADMAN:
The name of Allah be about you and the perfection of your ankles. Gazelles would die of jealousy at the sight of them.

PERFECT LOVE [*puzzled*]:
And yet you say your ankle rings will never fit.

MADMAN:
Because they are too large, and far too rough, for ankles such as yours.

PERFECT LOVE:
Oh. I thought they were quite otherwise. Now, show me some bracelets.

[*She reveals an arm.*]

I am weary today, try them for me, please. What have you seen, young man?

[*She covers herself. She is ashamed.*]

I am maimed and webbed fingered, am I not? I have arms like a hippopotamus, have I not?

MADMAN [*nearly breathless and barely daring to look*]:
The name of Allah be upon you and upon those white curves and upon that child's wrist. My smallest bracelets, made for children, will gape outrageously above each slim transparency.

PERFECT LOVE [*to herself*]:
Then they were not right? [*Aloud*] Now show me some gold necklets and breastplates.

[*She pulls her outer veil aside from her chest.*]

MADMAN:
Cover them, cover them! Allah veil them!

PERFECT LOVE:
What? Will you not help me to try on the necklets and breastplates?

[*She covers herself.*]

It doesn't matter. I will ask you for something else. I am rough and hairy, am I not, with breasts like a buffalo cow? Or is the other rumor correct: that I am all bone, and dry like a salt fish, and as flat as a carpenter's bench?

MADMAN:
The name of Allah be upon you and upon the hidden beauty and upon the hidden fruit!

PERFECT LOVE:
Were they fooling me, then, when they told me I had the ugliest hidden things in the world? Oh, never mind. And have you any belts?

[*He brings her one and lays it at her feet.*]

No, no! Try it for me in Allah's name.

[*The* MADMAN *picks up the belt and stands behind her.*]

MADMAN:
Mistress, I cannot fit—

PERFECT LOVE:
I know. They say I am deformed, with a double hump behind and

a double hump in front, with a horrible belly and a back like a camel's. Is it not so?

MADMAN [*lowering the belt over her head to her waist as he speaks*]:
Mistress, although this belt was made for an infant princess, it is too large for a waist which casts no shadow, for a waist which would fill the heart of a scribe with despair when he was making the letter S, for a waist which should wither the branch of a ban tree from sheer spite, for a waist which would shame the pride of a young peacock, for a waist which would burn a bamboo stem—

PERFECT LOVE [*pulling away*]:
You surprise me, young man. They have never been very complimentary about my waist at home. Now, perhaps you could find me some earrings and a gold frontlet for my hair.

[*She lifts the veil from her face and leaves it lifted. The* MADMAN *is overawed.*]

I see, young man, you are struck dumb by my ugliness. My own father, when I was born, took one look and ordered every mirror hidden from me, for pity. So I've been spared; I've never seen myself. But I know from many repetitions that my face is a hideous thing, a parchment pitted with smallpox, a blind right eye and a bleared left, a stinking mouth with broken teeth, and a pair of cropped ears. They say my skin is scabby, my hair is broken and frayed, and that the invisible horrors of my interior are not to be named.

MADMAN:
The name of Allah be upon you and upon your great beauty, visible and invisible.

PERFECT LOVE:

Then you do not find me a horror?

MADMAN:

By Allah, no.

PERFECT LOVE:

You would not deceive me?

MADMAN:

Never.

PERFECT LOVE:

Alas, why does my father hate me so? For it is he who attributes all these horrors to my appearance, and all my life I have lived as he has named me—horrible, unwanted, and unloved. I am glad that you seem to think I am not so! I do not think my father wishes to deceive me; I imagine he must have a hallucination which casts an ugliness upon all he sees. But, whatever the reason, he so hates the sight of me that he is ready to sell me to a merchant of slaves.

MADMAN:

Who is your father?

PERFECT LOVE:

The Sheikh al-Islam, in person.

MADMAN:

Rather than sell you, would he not let me marry you?

PERFECT LOVE:

Young man, I thank you for your offer—it is a great kindness, but you don't know what you are saying. My father is a scrupulous man; as he thinks his daughter a repulsive monster, he would not willingly wed her to such a one as you.

MADMAN:
There must be some way.

PERFECT LOVE:
Listen, you might do worse than to try to gain his consent. I don't wish to be sold. Tomorrow morning, present yourself before my holy father, and after exchanging pleasant greetings and comments about the hotness and dryness of the day, ask him for my hand in marriage. He is certain to say,

[SHEIKH AL-ISLAM *approaches.*]

PERFECT LOVE AND SHEIKH AL-ISLAM:
May Allah preserve your youth, my son. My daughter is a creature altogether helpless; there is nothing to be done for her. She is crooked and hideous.

PERFECT LOVE:
But you must cry out, "I am content!"

PERFECT LOVE AND MADMAN:
I am content!

PERFECT LOVE:
He will go on,

PERFECT LOVE AND SHEIKH AL-ISLAM:
I thank you for that, my son, but my daughter is not for any strong and handsome youth. She is . . .

PERFECT LOVE:
But you must cry out,

MADMAN:
I am content!

[PERFECT LOVE *and her entourage depart. The* MADMAN *is left alone with* SHEIKH AL-ISLAM. *They are now at his palace.*]

I am content!

SHEIKH AL-ISLAM:
You force me to the pain of plain speech. If you were to marry my daughter, you would be wedding the most terrible monster of our time!

MADMAN:
I am content! I am content!

SHEIKH AL-ISLAM:
But, my poor boy, she is blind of one eye, her ears are cropped, she is lame and stinking, a dribbler, a pisser—

MADMAN:
I am content!

SHEIKH AL-ISLAM:
She is disgusting and vicious, snot nosed and forever farting—

MADMAN:
I am content! I am content!

SHEIKH AL-ISLAM:

She is bearded and flab bellied, she is short of an arm and has a club foot, her left eye is covered with a film, her nose is a mass of oily pimples, her face is one sieve of smallpox, her mouth a cesspit, her teeth a wreck, her interior organs are one mutilation, she is bald and incredibly scabby, she is a horror, an abomination of desolation!

MADMAN:

I am content! Spare yourself the task of description, for I will go on soliciting your daughter, no matter what you find to say of her. I have a taste for horrors, my lord, when they are such as afflict your honorable daughter. I can only repeat, I am content, content, content!

SHEIKH AL-ISLAM:

If you are determined to persist in this madness, I will give my slow consent. But you must sign a contract before witnesses that you will accept your bride with all her faults, and if you dare divorce her, you will pay a ransom of twenty thousand gold dinars.

[SHEIKH AL-ISLAM *departs. Strange wedding music begins, and a triangle sounds the hour.*]

MADMAN:

I agreed to these conditions and would have agreed to a thousand more. How can an obscure merchant have won such happiness? Is it really true that I am to rejoice and take my ease with all that beauty?

[*A* FIGURE *comes forward, limping, strangely shaped, veiled from head to toe.*]

There was no celebration, no wedding feast, but I could not have been happier, as I was counting down the moments until I could see that perfect beauty in all her glory. I made myself ready and, at the first civil moment, went bounding to my bride's bed.

[*He glances under the veil; the* FIGURE *gurgles and thrashes about. During the following lines, the* MADMAN *runs away, and* SHAHRYAR, *curious, comes forward and glances at the* FIGURE *under the veil. He retreats, frightened and puzzled, to* SCHEHEREZADE.]

Oh, horror of horrors! May you never see such a sight! I saw the most repulsive, the most deformed, the most disgusting, the most repugnant, the most grotesque creature of a nightmare. She was worse than the description which that lovely and wicked girl had given of her. She was a monster of malformation, a rag so full of horror that I should retch if I describe her even now. I had willingly, eagerly, madly married a nauseating compendium of all disgusts which have ever entered into the imagination of the damned! The next morning I fled that sorrowful place back to my shop. But no sooner was I there [*dancing music of* PERFECT LOVE *begins*] than I saw the maiden of love made perfect, the vision of desire who had cast me into hell, come smiling toward me in the middle of her slaves.

[PERFECT LOVE *and her entourage approach, dancing. Their dance is the same as before, only more aggressive, bolder, and longer.* PERFECT LOVE *strips off her exterior veil as she comes forward. The dance ends with the sound of the shop bell. Immediately, the triangle is struck, signaling the dawn. Everyone drops to the floor except* SHAHRYAR, *who comes forward, and two of the dancing girls, who are revealed as* SCHEHEREZADE *and* DUNYAZADE. SHAHRYAR *holds his knife to* SCHEHEREZADE's *throat. The* WAZIR *stands, holding* SCHEHEREZADE's *shroud. We are back in the palace of* SHAHRYAR.]

SHAHRYAR:
Why have you stopped?

SCHEHEREZADE:
It is dawn, my lord.

DUNYAZADE:
Oh, Sister, if the king kills you now, he will never understand the Madman!

SCHEHEREZADE:
Perhaps if I were to live another day—but I see from the window that my father is already waiting with my shroud.

SHAHRYAR [*after a pause*]:
By Allah! He may wait another day.

SCHEHEREZADE:
May I not speak to him?

SHAHRYAR:
No!

[*He leaves.* SCHEHEREZADE *frantically studies her Book of Tales.*]

CHORUS:
The king departed to sit in judgment, raising some to office and lowering others, until the fall of day. But when the second night had come, she said,

[SHAHRYAR *returns and holds his knife to* SCHEHEREZADE's *throat.*]

SCHEHEREZADE:
And standing in the entrance of the shop the woman said,

PERFECT LOVE:
May this be a day of benediction, O bridegroom! May Allah put a crown upon your happiness! May joy abide with you!

PERFECT LOVE AND HER WOMEN:
May joy abide with you and your new wife!

MADMAN:
You cauldron of pitch! You wicked girl! You bowl of tar! You are not the daughter of Sheikh al-Islam!

PERFECT LOVE:
No. No more than you.

MADMAN:
May Allah curse the hour of our meeting, may he damn the foul blackness of your soul! Why have you done this, you wanton whore? Why have you tricked me and destroyed my life?

PERFECT LOVE:
What is all of this, Sounding Brass? Have you forgotten the ode I wrote and sent to you so many years ago, and your great virtue, and my poor little slave?

[*The shop bell rings. The* SLAVE GIRL *enters.*]

MADMAN:
What?

[PERFECT LOVE *begins to sing mournfully, accompanied by music. As she sings, all the* WOMEN *dance and sing in counterrythym.*]

WOMEN [*singing repeatedly under* PERFECT LOVE]:
O merchant, you should have listened when Perfect Love first came to call.

[*The* SHOP ASSISTANT *recovers the torn-up pieces of the ode and lets them fall slowly from his hand.*]

PERFECT LOVE [*singing*]:
Love has filled my soul with wine and gold
But I keep them for you
Who has put the black scorpions of your hair
To feed upon my soul.

Come with me to the bath, beloved,
And I will lie, singing, on your heart.

[PERFECT LOVE'*s song ends. She turns to go.*]

Farewell.

MADMAN:
Please, don't go! In truth, I repent!

PERFECT LOVE:
Too late.

MADMAN:
I see clearly now how gross and foolish was my conduct toward you

and your little slave, how vulgar and hypocritical, how full of stupid vanity and—and—

PERFECT LOVE:
Unfounded pride?

MADMAN:
Please excuse me, mistress. It was so many years ago. Pardon me this once, this once, please.

[*The* SHOP ASSISTANT *kneels in supplication. Slowly, the other* WOMEN *kneel down. Finally, the little* SLAVE GIRL *kneels.*]

PERFECT LOVE:
I will pardon you this once, but you must promise never to do the like again.

MADMAN:
O mistress, Perfect Love, I kneel in your protection and look for deliverance at your hands.

PERFECT LOVE:
I have already thought of that. Since I'm the one who caught you, it is only right that I should set you free.

MADMAN:
But how? I've signed a contract—

PERFECT LOVE:
Listen carefully, and you will soon be free of that unfortunate girl. First, you must go to the foot of the citadel and call together all the

acrobats, quacks, idiots, dancers, rope walkers, tambourines, cymbals, clarinets, and funny men that you find there. Then you must go back to the house of Sheikh al-Islam . . .

[PERFECT LOVE *departs;* SHEIKH AL-ISLAM *comes forward. The* FOOLS *are approaching in the distance.*]

SHEIKH AL-ISLAM:
I must say I never expected my daughter to find such happiness.

MADMAN:
She is happiness itself.

SHEIKH AL-ISLAM:
You see her mother was frightened by a fire and delivered her before her time.

MADMAN:
She was delivered in perfect time for me.

SHEIKH AL-ISLAM:
Well, I really must say that I never expected—did you hear something?

MADMAN:
No.

SHEIKH AL-ISLAM:
Well, as I was saying—

[*The* FOOLS *enter with great fanfare. They shout, tumble, run about, piss on the floor, and generally misbehave.*]

PRINCE OF FOOLS:
Greetings, Sheikh al-Islam! May Allah's blessing be upon you! In the name of all your new family, I wish you prosperity!

SHEIKH AL-ISLAM [*outraged*]:
Who are these people?

PRINCE OF FOOLS [*to the* MADMAN]:
O Cousin, know that we will never, ever desert you!

SHEIKH AL-ISLAM:
You know these people?

PRINCE OF FOOLS:
And as you have made this your new home, so it is ours as well. Forever and ever and ever and ever!

SHEIKH AL-ISLAM:
Are you the son of a quack? Are these vile gypsies kin to you?

MADMAN:
Because I love your daughter and her honor, I cannot deny my birth and family. Blood remembers blood. Now, come on! Let's do the family dance!

FOOLS:
The family dance!

[*They dance madly, stupidly.*]

SHEIKH AL-ISLAM:
Young man! Your marriage contract is illegal! You falsified your parentage!

MADMAN:
Let's do the family dance!

[*They dance.*]

SHEIKH AL-ISLAM:
No, we will not do the family dance! You cannot remain in the house of Sheikh al-Islam! You cannot remain married to my daughter!

MADMAN:
Oh, no! I have won her and will not divorce her for all the kingdom of Iraq!

SHEIKH AL-ISLAM:
You shall divorce her!

MADMAN:
But every one of her hairs is more precious to me than a thousand lives!

FOOLS:
The family dance!

SHEIKH AL-ISLAM [*pleading*]:
Please. Protect my honor, and Allah will surely protect yours.

MADMAN:
By Allah! I will not remain in the home of one who does not love my family. Here, in front of witnesses, I put away your daughter. I put her away once, twice, three times!

SHEIKH AL-ISLAM:
And thus an end to this unfortunate business!

[*The* FOOLS *and the* SHEIKH *depart.* PERFECT LOVE *and the* MADMAN *meet.*]

PERFECT LOVE:
Shall we come together now, dear master?

MADMAN:
In your house or at my shop?

PERFECT LOVE:
Poor lad, don't you know that a woman has many preparations before such things can be? We'll go to my house.

MADMAN:
But my shop is large enough to hold us both, and if in love we burn it to the ground, there is still the vast chamber of my heart.

PERFECT LOVE:
Your compliments have improved in quality with the years.

MADMAN:
Let's hurry. I feel the wasted days clamor within me.

PERFECT LOVE:
Ah, ah, ah! Before the fight, O soldier, let me hear if you know the name of your antagonist.

[*She points to the spot between her legs. The triangle chimes, signaling the dawn.* PERFECT LOVE *and the* MADMAN *are still. We are back in the palace of* SHAHRYAR. *The* WAZIR *stands apart, holding the shroud of* SCHEHEREZADE.]

SHAHRYAR:
You're stopping now?

SCHEHEREZADE:
It is dawn, my lord. My father has returned with my shroud.

SHAHRYAR:
Let him wait another day. Tonight you will finish this story and then die.

[*He departs.*]

CHORUS:
The king departed to sit in judgment, raising some to office and lowering others, until the fall of day. But when the third night had come, she said,

SCHEHEREZADE AND PERFECT LOVE:
Before the fight, O soldier, let me hear if you know the name of your antagonist.

MADMAN [*guessing*]:
River of grace?

PERFECT LOVE:
No.

MADMAN:
White feather?

PERFECT LOVE:
No.

MADMAN:
Sweet fleshy?

PERFECT LOVE:
No.

MADMAN:
Peeled sesame?

PERFECT LOVE:
No.

MADMAN:
Basil of the bridge?

PERFECT LOVE:
No.

MADMAN:
Wild mule?

PERFECT LOVE:
You are wrong. Did your masters teach you nothing at school?

MADMAN:
Nothing.

PERFECT LOVE [*approaching him*]:
Then listen to the thing's rightful names. They are: dumb starling, fat sheep, silent tongue, wordless eloquence, adjustable vice, sliding rule, mad biter, great shaker, magnetic gulf, Jacob's well, little cradle,

nest without eggs, bird without feathers, dove without stain, cat without whiskers, silent chicken, and rabbit without ears.

MADMAN:
Where shall I begin?

PERFECT LOVE:
Where you like.

[*They come together.*]

MADMAN:
Then I say to the child of my inheritance: Feed the starling!

PERFECT LOVE:
Allah increase you! Allah increase you!

MADMAN:
Bow to the sweet fat sheep.

PERFECT LOVE:
Allah increase you! Allah increase you!

MADMAN:
Now speak to the silent tongue.

PERFECT LOVE:
Allah increase you! Allah increase you!

MADMAN:
Now tame the savage biter's bite.

PERFECT LOVE:
A right drink, a right, a drink of delight!

MADMAN:
Now heat the bird without feathers.

PERFECT LOVE:
Now I am warm for all weathers.

MADMAN:
Now give corn to the dumb chick.

PERFECT LOVE:
A benediction! Oh, benedic, dic, dic!

MADMAN:
Don't forget the rabbit without an ear. It has fallen fast asleep, I fear.

PERFECT LOVE [*sighing*]:
I hear. I hear.

SCHEHEREZADE:
Life and love lived love and life together for thirty days and nights, my lord,

SCHEHEREZADE AND MADMAN:
until a giddiness came over me, and I dared to say,

MADMAN:
I don't know why, my saint, but I can't do it again today.

PERFECT LOVE:
But the twelfth time is the most important, the first eleven don't count!

MADMAN:
Yet it is impossible. Impossible.

PERFECT LOVE:
Then you must have rest, my poor, you must have rest.

MADMAN:
When I heard that, I lay down and fainted clear away [SCHEHER-EZADE *comes forward, puts the chains around his neck; we are back in the madhouse, with* HARUN AL-RASHID, JAFAR, *et al., and* PERFECT LOVE *is there as well*] and woke up in these chains, fastened to the wall of this madhouse. I asked the chief of keys, "Why am I here?"

CHIEF OF KEYS:
You must have rest. The young woman said,

PERFECT LOVE:
He must have rest.

HARUN AL-RASHID:
Even if you had been chained here for madness, I would have freed you for the sake of this story. Young lady, I know the trouble that was between you in the past, but I take it upon myself that such a thing shall not happen again. The lad is well rested and ready for anything.

PERFECT LOVE:
I hear and I obey. I am prepared to live with him again.

HARUN AL-RASHID:
I thank you, my child. You have lifted a great weight from my heart.

[HARUN AL-RASHID *and* JAFAR *depart.*]

SCHEHEREZADE:
They lived together in all delight, and the practice of every virtue, knowing days each more admirable than the last, and nights whiter than the days [*sound of wind comes up*] until they were visited by the destroyer of joy, the separator of friends, and died.

[*The two lie down together, roll across the floor as if pushed by the wind, and stop. The triangle sounds. The* WAZIR *stands, holding the shroud.*]

But glory be to he the living, who dies not, who reigns over the visible and invisible world.

SHAHRYAR:
By Allah, I will remember that story.

[*A pause. Then* SHAHRYAR *rushes at her with his knife.*]

SCHEHEREZADE:
My king! It is early yet!

SHAHRYAR:
What of it?

SCHEHEREZADE:
Let me make the darkness gentle for you. There will be time to kill me with the dawn.

[*Pause.*]

SHAHRYAR:
Tell me, do you know any moral anecdotes?

SCHEHEREZADE:
Moral anecdotes, O auspicious king, are the tales which I know best.
I could tell you one or two or three from the perfumed garden—

SHAHRYAR:
Begin quickly, for a great weariness weighs upon my soul tonight,
and I doubt whether your head is safe upon your shoulders.

SCHEHEREZADE:
Listen, then. But first I must warn you that although these anecdotes are very moral, some of them might seem licentious or lewd
to those with gross and narrow minds.

SHAHRYAR:
Don't let that stop you. But if you think these tales may be unfit for
this little one [*pointing his knife at* DUNYAZADE] who listens—I do
not very well know why—among the carpets at our feet, send her
away at once.

SCHEHEREZADE:
I think she should be allowed to stay, for "to the pure and clean all
things are pure and clean," and there is nothing shameful in speaking of those things which lie below our waists.

SHAHRYAR:
Begin at once.

[HARUN AL-RASHID *and his* JESTER *come forward.*]

SCHEHEREZADE:
It is related, O auspicious king, that a certain jester lived at the court of Harun al-Rashid.

[*The finger cymbals ring once. The* JESTER *is at the end of his joke and may offer a different punch line if he likes.*]

JESTER:
. . . and so the camel said to the merchant, "And with prices like these, you won't be getting many more."

HARUN AL-RASHID [*not amused*]:
You are a bachelor, are you not?

JESTER [*slowly*]:
Yes.

HARUN AL-RASHID:
Yes. Well, I have conceived a keen—

JESTER:
Don't say it—

HARUN AL-RASHID:
desire to—

JESTER:
No, no—

HARUN AL-RASHID:
see you married.

JESTER [*kneeling*]:
King of Time, I pray you, spare me that felicity. I am a bachelor
through fear of the sex; I have abstained so that I may never happen
upon some debauched, adulterous, whoring woman. I pray you to
think of all my faults and all the ignoble qualities of my life and, as
a punishment for them, deny me the blessing of matrimony.

HARUN AL-RASHID:
Well, I can't help your feelings. Today you must be married.

JESTER:
It's just that I—

HARUN AL-RASHID:
Today!

JESTER:
All right! All right! All right!

[*A modest-seeming young bride, the* JESTER'S WIFE, *approaches.*
HARUN AL-RASHID *departs.*]

SCHEHEREZADE:
For half a year, or maybe seven months, the jester lived at peace
with his new bride, a beautiful and modest-seeming girl, but after
that there happened that which was fated to happen, for no man can
escape his destiny.

JESTER:
I have been invited to go out into the gardens this afternoon to take
the good air with my friends.

JESTER'S WIFE [*collapsing in tears*]:
Oh, no!

JESTER:
If you want me for anything, you will know where to send.

JESTER'S WIFE [*bravely stifling her tears*]:
No one will want you to do anything but enjoy yourself. If you take a delight in the gardens, it will be an equal delight for me.

JESTER:
Farewell.

JESTER'S WIFE:
Farewell, my sweet.

JESTER:
Farewell.

JESTER'S WIFE:
Farewell, my love.

JESTER:
Farewell.

[*He goes.*]

JESTER'S WIFE [*ripping off her veil*]:
Praise Allah! I've gotten rid of that wild pig for one afternoon! Now I will send for my heart's delight!

[*A knock sounds at the door.*]

Who can that be? Not that dog of a husband back again, I hope.

[*The* PASTRYCOOK *appears. He is covered in flour, wears an apron, and carries a rolling pin. Music.*]

O my pastrycook!

PASTRYCOOK:
My tart!

JESTER'S WIFE:
You are earlier than usual.

PASTRYCOOK:
I am. When I had prepared my dough and rolled it and leavened it and stuffed it with almonds and pistachios, I noticed that it was still too early for customers to be dropping by. So I said to myself: Shake the flour from your clothes, my friend, and go to rejoice a little with your sweet!

[*She leaps on him. They run around shouting and twirling in a wild frenzy.*]

The dough is rising! The dough is rising!

[*There is a knock at the door. The music ends.*]

Who can that be?

JESTER'S WIFE:
I don't know. Go and hide yourself in the privy while I see.

[*The* PASTRYCOOK *hides. The* GREENGROCER *appears. He has a basket of long vegetables. Music.*]

O my greengrocer! You are a little too soon!

GREENGROCER:
That's right. But as I was returning from my kitchen garden this morning, I thought, You had better take your fresh vegetables, your heroic cucumber, your exceptional pumpkin, and your embarrassing butternut to your sweet, for they will rejoice her!

[*They leap on each other, madly happy.*]

Climb my vine! Climb my vine! Reap and sow! Reap and sow!

[*There is a knock at the door. The music ends.*]

Who's there?

JESTER'S WIFE:
I don't know! Go and hide in the privy while I see.

GREENGROCER [*entering the privy and finding the* PASTRYCOOK]:
Who are you? Why are you here?

PASTRYCOOK:
I've been doing what you've been doing, and I'm in here for the same reason as yourself!

[*They hide. The* BUTCHER *appears with a lambskin. Music.*]

JESTER'S WIFE:
My sweet butcher!

BUTCHER:
My sweet meat!

JESTER'S WIFE:
You are too soon!

BUTCHER:
When I had finished slaughtering all my lambs for the day, I thought, You had better take your sweet this sheepskin; it will be a soft carpet for her head, and she will start her morning well for you! Bleat for me!

[*They begin to roll around, playing, making little farm-animal noises. There is a knock at the door. The music ends.*]

Who's that?

JESTER'S WIFE:
Quick! Take your sheepskin and hide in the privy!

[*He does so. The* CLARINETIST *appears with his instrument, flexing his muscles. Music.*]

O my clarinet player! You are too soon!

CLARINETIST:
When I went to my rehearsal today, none of the other players had come and so I determined to wait in the dwelling of my sweet! Come here my little piccolo!

[*He chases her around; she shrieks in delight.*]

We seem to be a little flat today, just a little flat! Come now! Let's moisten our reed!

[*He catches her and starts to spank her as she spanks him in turn. There is a knock at the door. The music ends.*]

Who is that?

JESTER'S WIFE:
Allah alone knows! Perhaps it is my husband! Take your clarinet and hide yourself in the privy!

CLARINETIST [*at the privy*]:
Peace be with you, friends! What are you doing in this singular apartment?

PASTRYCOOK, GREENGROCER, AND BUTCHER:
Peace be with you, friend! Same thing as yourself!

[*They hide; the* JESTER *enters.*]

JESTER:
Give me an infusion of anise and fennel, good wife! Things are moving! Things are moving! I couldn't stay at the garden any longer. I had to come home to relieve my—

[*He opens the door to the privy. Everything stops.*]

SCHEHEREZADE:
The jester realized at once the exact nature of his predicament. But

what if these four lovers should turn on him and kill him to hide their crime? He decided to try a trick.

JESTER [*bowing to the ground*]:
O sacred messengers of Allah, I know you, I recognize you well! You who are all white and floury might be mistaken for a pastrycook by the profane, but you are without doubt the holy patriarch Job, the ulcerous. And you, O saint with the box of excellent vegetables, must be the great Khidr, who guards each orchard, who clothes each tree with a green diadem. And you, with the lion's skin, surely you are Cleopatra, queen of the Nile! And you, you, O glorious angel with the heavenly horn, are certainly Israfil, who shall summon us on the last day!

PASTRYCOOK [*terrified but assuming a divine air*]:
You are not mistaken, O man! We are even as you have named us, and we have come to earth through your privy because we wished to enter your house and reward you for your great virtue.

BUTCHER [*following suit*]:
We could find no other chamber open to the sky.

JESTER:
Since you have done me the honor of this visit, O illustrious saints, will you grant me one wish?

PASTRYCOOK, GREENGROCER, BUTCHER, AND CLARINETIST:
Speak! Speak!

JESTER:
Come with me to the palace of Harun al-Rashid. He will be greatly obliged when I introduce four such famous visitors to him.

GREENGROCER [*caught up in the glory of it all*]:
We shall grant you that particular grace!

[*There is a little parade to the palace. The lovers are frightened. Some funereal music.* HARUN AL-RASHID *comes forward.*]

JESTER:
O my lord. Allow me to present to you four sacred personages: our lord Job; our lord Khidr; Cleopatra, queen of the Nile; and the angel Israfil, who shall announce the Last Judgment. I found them in my privy, my lord, and I owe the great honor of their visit to the saintly qualities of the wife whom you so generously gave to me.

HARUN AL-RASHID:
Have you gone mad or are you trying to kill me?

JESTER:
I only tell you what I have seen.

HARUN AL-RASHID:
Do you not see that the prophet Job is a pastrycook, the prophet Khidr is a greengrocer, the queen of the Nile is a butcher, and the angel Israfil is my first clarinet, the master of my music?

JESTER:
I only tell you what I have seen.

HARUN AL-RASHID:
Sons and daughter of a thousand shameless horns! Tell me the truth: you are the lovers of that wife of his!

PASTRYCOOK, GREENGROCER, BUTCHER, AND CLARINETIST:
Well, we . . . it seems . . .

HARUN AL-RASHID:
On your knees, dogs! O Father of Wisdom, I grant you your divorce! A curse on all women! And you, you lovers, shall have your
eggs torn from you. I've never heard such a story in all my life!
Guards!

SCHEHEREZADE [*coming forward to join the* PASTRYCOOK]:
But, quick as lightning, the pastrycook came forward, kissed the
ground, and said,

SCHEHEREZADE AND PASTRYCOOK:
O most auspicious king, if I tell you a story more wonderful still
than the story of our adventure in the house of this honorable man
perhaps you may see your way clear to sparing my eggs?

SCHEHEREZADE:
And the honorable Harun al-Rashid said,

HARUN AL-RASHID:
It is permitted.

SCHEHEREZADE:
And the pastrycook began at once the story of "The Dream."

[*The finger cymbals ring once. The following might be staged with
the company asleep in a row on the floor, changing positions in
sleep every now and then. The various characters—the* POOR MAN,
the MAN IN THE DREAM, *the* THIEVES, *the* FAMILY, *and the rest—rise
from this line when they speak, cross over one another when they*

move, and sink back into sleep when they are done. They some-times speak as a chorus, in their sleep.]

PASTRYCOOK:

It is related, but Allah is all wise and all knowing, that one night in Baghdad, a poor man lay down to sleep. While some in the city had fine carpets, and some in the city had fine palaces and fine pillows for their heads, he had only the bare floor in his little hut at the end of a cobbled street lined with palm trees and a gray stone courtyard containing a dry and cracked little fountain with a design of birds upon it. All of us are equal in our sleep, and in our sleep all of us may speak to God and hear our destiny revealed. This night the poor man lay down with a heavy heart, and a man came to him in a dream.

MAN IN THE DREAM:

My poor man, know that your fortune lies far away in Cairo. Go and seek it there.

CHORUS [*turning in their sleep*]:
Your fortune lies far away in Cairo. Go and seek it there.

PASTRYCOOK:

The very next morning the poor man set out for Cairo, and after many weeks and much hardship, he arrived in that city.

CHORUS [*turning in their sleep*]:
Night fell. He could not afford to stay at an inn, so he lay down to sleep in the courtyard of a mosque.

THIEVES:

That night robbers entered the mosque and from there broke into an adjoining house.

FAMILY:
Awakened by the noise, the owners raised the alarm and called for help.

POLICE:
The police arrived, found the poor man from Baghdad, beat him, and threw him into jail.

PASTRYCOOK:
Three days later, the chief of police ordered his men to bring the stranger before him.

CHIEF OF POLICE:
Where do you come from?

POOR MAN:
I come from Baghdad.

CHIEF OF POLICE:
And what brought you to Cairo?

POOR MAN:
A man came to me in a dream, saying,

POOR MAN AND MAN IN THE DREAM:
My poor man, your fortune lies far away in Cairo. Go and seek it there.

POOR MAN:
But when I came to Cairo, the fortune I was promised proved to be the beating your men so generously gave me.

CHIEF OF POLICE:
What a fool to believe in dreams! Know this: I too have heard a voice in my sleep, not just once but three times. It said,

CHIEF OF POLICE AND PASTRYCOOK:
Go to Baghdad and find a little hut at the end of a cobbled street lined with palm trees and a gray stone courtyard containing a dry and cracked little fountain with a design of birds upon it. Under that old fountain a great sum of money lies buried. Go there and dig it up.

CHIEF OF POLICE:
But did I go? Of course not! Yet fool that you are, you have come all the way to Cairo on the strength of one idle dream. Here, take this.

[*He tosses the* POOR MAN *a coin.*]

It will help you on your way back to your own country.

PASTRYCOOK:
The poor man recognized at once that the house and garden described in the dream of the chief of police were his own. He took the money and set out promptly on his homeward journey.

CHORUS [*turning in their sleep*]:
Go on back to Baghdad, City of Peace and Poets. Your fortune is in the garden of your home.

PASTRYCOOK:
As soon as he reached his house he went into the garden, dug beneath the fountain, and uncovered a great treasure.

CHORUS:
Your fortune is in the garden of your home.

PASTRYCOOK:
And thus the words of the dream were wondrously fulfilled.

CHORUS [*turning in their sleep*]:
Your fortune is in the garden of your home and speaks to you in dreams.

[*The scene dissolves back to the court of* HARUN AL-RASHID.]

HARUN AL-RASHID:
That is an excellent tale indeed, Pastrycook, if it is true. But whether it is true or not, I do pardon you.

SCHEHEREZADE:
With that the butcher came forward, kissed the ground, and said,

SCHEHEREZADE AND BUTCHER:
Most excellent king, grant me the same favor as my colleague the pastrycook, and I will tell you an even fairer tale—a tale that may inspire you to generous deeds.

HARUN AL-RASHID:
It is permitted.

SCHEHEREZADE:
And the butcher began the tale of "The Contest of Generosity."

[*The finger cymbals ring once.*]

SCHEHEREZADE AND BUTCHER:
It is related—but Allah is all wise and all knowing—that there was once in the city of Baghdad a boy and a girl who loved each other from infancy.

BOY AND GIRL [*chanting and dancing as children*]:
Cool is the night in the Rabwah Valley
Where the rivers give and the breezes carry
It's ringed with flowers where we'll marry
When evening comes, the moon will yield
Silver to work in the carpets of her fields,
And every single night we'll sing

eight, nine, ten.

[*The* BOY *and* GIRL *are a little older now. They repeat the poem with growing sophistication, ending with:*]

. . . eleven, twelve, thirteen.

[*They repeat the poem, more slowly, with growing intimacy, and end with:*]

. . . fourteen, fifteen, sixteen.

[*They are grown now. They are about to kiss.*]

BUTCHER:
But as they grew, the fortune of the boy's family rose while that of the girl's fell.

GIRL:
Beloved cousin, have you heard? My father and mother are forced to marry me to a sheikh that I've never seen. Beloved, had you heard?

BOY:
No.

GIRL:
I must leave tonight.

BOY:
Then you must go now. It's growing dark.

GIRL:
What do you mean? It is midday. Can't you see the sun?

BOY:
No. It's growing dark.

GIRL:
What do you see?

BOY:
Nothing. The sun wakes in your eyes, and the moon sleeps in the hollow of your throat. I've heard that you are going and I am growing blind from grief.

GIRL:
Say what's in your heart.

BOY:
A desert.

BUTCHER:
And so she said,

BUTCHER AND GIRL:
As the poet says,

GIRL [*with music*]:
When you passed on by my tent door
I said goodbye to all the world,
Forgetting how to love forevermore
When you passed on.

If you come back the way you went
I pray you take my body up,
And set it in a calm grave near your tent
When you come back.

If your dear voice recalls the tones
The sweetness of the way you said my name,
Kneel down, dear love, and say the same;
I'll answer with the clicking of my bones.

Farewell.

[*She travels to the home of the wealthy* SHEIKH. *The* BOY *begins to sing, alone.*]

BOY:
Farewell cheeks of surface silver,
Golden wrists with copper bangles,
Lake hair lying in black angles.

Dreams are pictures in the book of sleep
And no more mine
And no more mine forever.

[*The* SHEIKH *enters. The* GIRL *is crying beneath a blanket.*]

SHEIKH:
Surely my new bride weeps as young girls do, because she has left her mother. Happily, this does not last long. A kind word will cure her.

[*He approaches the* GIRL.]

O light of my soul, why do you destroy the beauty of your eyes? Dear girl, if you are crying for your mother, say so, and I will fetch her to you instantly.

[*She only cries.*]

If you are crying for your father, or one of your sisters, or your nurse, or some pet animal, such as a rooster, a cat, or a gazelle, tell me, and you shall no longer be separated from your desire.

[*She cries louder.*]

Is it the house itself for which you weep, the house where you were young? I'll take you back there at once.

GIRL [*revealing herself*]:
My lord, I do not weep for my mother, my father, my sisters, my nurse, or my pets; and I beg you not to insist that I tell you the reason.

SHEIKH:
Fairest girl on earth, then I know what it is; you cry because I am repugnant to you.

GIRL:
No, by Allah, I have no aversion to you. It's something else.

SHEIKH:
What then?

GIRL:
My grief and tears are for a dear one of my house, a cousin with
whom I grew up, a cousin who loves me and whom I love. O master,
love's roots are in the heart, and if love is torn away, then the heart
is torn away also.

BUTCHER:
The sheikh lowered his head and reflected for an hour.

SHEIKH:
Dear mistress, the law of Allah and his Prophet (upon whom be
prayer and peace) forbids one Believer to snatch even a mouthful of
bread from another by force. How then could I snatch away your
heart? Rise up, my bride of a minute, and go with my full consent to
your cousin. Give yourself to him and return here in the morning
before the servants are awake. From now on this is how we shall
live. You are as my daughter.

GIRL:
A blessing be upon you.

[*Music as she travels.*]

BUTCHER:
She left that good man's house, glowing in the night in her happiness and her wedding jewels, but she had barely gone twenty paces when—

ROBBER [*jumping forward*]:
By Allah! My lucky night! Nothing for six weeks and now a wedding guest in all her jewels!

[*He stalks her as she counts her steps under her breath. Then he attacks.*]

Give me all your jewels, or I'll smash you to the earth.

[*He sees her face.*]

As Allah lives! You are the richest jewel of all. I'll have you whole. Dear mistress, I will do you no harm if you are complacent, and I can promise you a most blessed night if you come with me.

GIRL:
Oh, no!

ROBBER:
I swear I will neither hurt you nor rob you if you give yourself to me freely. But you must stop that crying!

GIRL:
Just when everything was going so well!

ROBBER:
What's that you say?

GIRL:
Just when everything was going so well, and I was going to the home of the one I love!

ROBBER:
What wedding were you at?

GIRL:
My own! My parents were forced to marry me to a sheikh I'd never seen, but I've loved my cousin since infancy. When I explained this to the sheikh, the good man let me go.

ROBBER:
He let you go?

GIRL:
Yes, he told me to consummate a marriage with my cousin and return to his house as his daughter.

ROBBER:
He did that?

GIRL:
Yes.

ROBBER:
He let you go, just like that?

GIRL:
Yes. But now I have fallen into your hands. A thief is not like a sheikh. [*Despairingly*] Do with me as you will.

ROBBER [*sighs*]:
Where does he live, this cousin whom you love?

GIRL:
In a room on a garden in such and such a house on such and such a
street.

ROBBER:
Dear mistress, no one shall ever accuse a man of my profession of
interfering with the course of true love. I will now lead you to your
cousin's house, as you might fall in with some vile thief if you were
to go alone. The wind is for all, the flute is for one, and that one is
not I.

BUTCHER:
So saying, he took the girl by the hand and escorted her, as if she
had been a queen, up to the house of her beloved.

[*Music. They travel. The* GIRL *approaches her* COUSIN *from behind
and covers his eyes.*]

BOY:
By Allah! I can see! Who's hands are these?

GIRL:
Beloved?

BOY:
Who are you to speak to me in the voice of my—

GIRL:
Your cousin.

BOY:
Cousin! What have you done? How have you—?

BUTCHER:
She explained to him all of her adventures on this strange night—

[SHAHRYAR *is impatient and signals* SCHEHEREZADE *to get on with it.*]

BUTCHER AND SCHEHEREZADE:
but nothing would be gained by repeating it in this place.

BOY:
What a generous man, this sheikh! Great deeds inspire greater deeds. Cousin, there is only one thing we can do. I must return you to this saint, untouched.

GIRL:
What?

BOY:
Cousin, do you agree?

GIRL [*nodding*]:
In the face of such virtue, what else can we do?

[*Music. They travel quickly to the* SHEIKH.]

SHEIKH:
Children, don't tell me why you are here—I have already guessed. But you must know this: when a Believer has claimed his wife to be the daughter of his flesh and blood, no power can give lie to his

words. You owe me nothing, my children. I am in bondage to my oath.

BUTCHER:
So saying, that good man gave his house and all his goods to the two of them and went to live in another city.

[*The* SHEIKH *departs. Then the* BUTCHER, *the* ROBBER, *and the* LOVER *line up in front of* SHAHRYAR.]

SCHEHEREZADE [*to* SHAHRYAR]:
Now, Prince of Time, let us stop and consider. Who was the most generous? The lover, the thief, or the husband?

SHAHRYAR:
They're all idiots.

SCHEHEREZADE:
Then we'll judge for ourselves.

[*She holds a handkerchief over each one's head. Everyone claps for his or her favorite and encourages the audience to vote as well.*]

Was it the lover? The thief? Or was it the husband?

[*She gives the handkerchief to the winner, which is usually the* SHEIKH. *The finger cymbals ring, and we are back in the court of* HARUN AL-RASHID.]

HARUN AL-RASHID:
That was an edifying tale indeed. I pardon you, Butcher.

SCHEHEREZADE:
At that, the greengrocer came forward, kissed the ground, and said,

SCHEHEREZADE AND GREENGROCER:
No disrespect to my colleagues the pastrycook and the butcher, but
I too have a tale, concerning a Kurd and a Persian, that may delight
your honorable majesty.

HARUN AL-RASHID [*wearily*]:
It is permitted.

SCHEHEREZADE:
And the greengrocer began his tale of "The Wonderful Bag."

[*"The Wonderful Bag" may be improvised anew for each performance (see "Improvisation in 'The Wonderful Bag,'" page 133) or
played as follows.*]

GREENGROCER:
One day, in the marketplace of Baghdad, someone let fall a little bag
and walked on without noticing.

[*He throws the bag, a wretched little thing, in the air. As it falls,
there is a scuffle for it. The* PERSIAN *snatches the bag and starts to
leave.*]

KURD:
What are you doing trying to walk off with this bag as though it belonged to you ever since you were born?

PERSIAN:
O Mussulmen, save my goods from this wretched unbeliever who
wishes to make off with my bag!

64

KURD:

My bag is known and well known. It is universally acknowledged to be my bag!

[*The* KADI *enters.*]

KADI:

Hold on here! Who is the plaintiff and who the defendant?

[*He takes the bag from the* PERSIAN.]

PERSIAN:

Allah increase the power of our kadi and judge! This bag is my bag. I lost it and found it again in the street today!

KADI:

When did you lose it?

PERSIAN:

I lost it yesterday, and I could not sleep all night for thinking of it.

KURD:

May Allah lift up and honor our master the kadi. I lost that bag two weeks ago and have not slept for thinking of it since.

KADI:

The truth can be uncovered soon enough! Whoever is the true owner of the bag shall best be able to describe its contents. Each of you give a list, and whoever's list is closest to a true inventory of the contents shall own the bag and everything in it.

KURD:

O Kadi, there are in my bag two crystal flasks filled with kohl, two silver sticks for putting on this kohl, a handkerchief, two lemonade glasses with gilded rims, two torches, two ladles, a cushion, two carpets for gaming tables, two water pots, two basins, one dish, one cook pot, one large knitting needle, a rice jar, a pregnant cat, two donkeys, two bedroom sets for women, a linen garment, a cow, two calves, a sheep with two lambs, two racing dromedaries, a lioness, a female bear, one couch, two beds, a palace with two reception halls, a kitchen with two doors, and an assembly of Kurds of my own kind all ready to swear that this bag is my bag.

PERSIAN:

O Kadi, let me say that in this bag are only a ruined pavilion, a house without a kitchen, a large dog kennel, a boys' school, some happy young men playing dice, a robber's lair, an army with captains, the city of Basrah and the city of Baghdad, a fishing net, a walnut, four chess players, two long swords, two hares, a blind man and two far-seeing men, a ship with sailors, a Christian priest and two deacons, twelve untouched girls, and a kadi and two witnesses ready to bear witness that this bag is my bag.

KURD:

I ought to add that, in this bag, besides the things I've mentioned, there are headache cures, spells and enchantments, coats of mail and armories filled with arms, a thousand rams trained for fighting, a deer park, men who love women, boy fanciers, gardens filled with trees and flowers, vines loaded with grapes, apples and figs, shades and phantoms, newly married couples with all their marriage fresh about them, cries and jokes, twelve disgraceful odors, some friends sitting in a meadow, banners and flags, a bride coming out of the bath, three Indian women, four Greek women, fifty Turkish women, seventy Persian women, the land of Iraq the Earthly Paradise, two stables, a mosque, many hammams, a hundred merchants, a plank, a nail, a red-haired man playing the clarinet, the city of Kufah, and—may Allah preserve the days of our mater the kadi—a shroud, a coffin, and a razor for the beard of the kadi if the kadi does not recognize my rights and say that this bag is my bag!

KADI:
As Allah lives, either you are two rascals mocking at the law and its representatives, or this bag is a bottomless abyss or the Valley of the Day of Judgment itself. Let us see what is in the bag.

[*He empties it onto the floor.*]

A little orange rind and some olive stones.

PERSIAN AND KURD [*variously*]:
All right, it's yours.

[*The finger cymbals ring. We are back at the palace of* HARUN AL-RASHID.]

HARUN AL-RASHID:
That is possibly the single most absurd story I have ever heard.

[*The triangle is struck.*]

SHAHRYAR:
This is the most absurd story I have ever heard as well. That bag is barely the size of your head! Who could believe so small a space could contain . . .

[*Here* SHAHRYAR *quotes a couple of items from the lists.*]

SCHEHEREZADE:
But in our heads, my lord, we do contain all the images of the universe—

SHAHRYAR:
Impossible!

[*He contemptuously mutters an item from the lists—the most absurd.*]

So, go on. What is your next tale? I hope it is more reasonable, or you shall soon lose your own wonderful bag.

[*He points at her throat with his knife.*]

SCHEHEREZADE:
Harun al-Rashid said,

SCHEHEREZADE AND HARUN AL-RASHID:
That is possibly the single most absurd story I have ever heard!

HARUN AL-RASHID:
I pardon you, Greengrocer!

SCHEHEREZADE:
With this, the clarinetist came forward, kissed the ground, and said,

SCHEHEREZADE AND CLARINETIST:
O Prince of Time! I have a story even more absurd—if you will hear it.

HARUN AL-RASHID:
It is permitted.

[*The finger cymbals ring.*]

CLARINETIST:
Perhaps you have heard, Harun al-Rashid, of the noble but most unfortunate Abu al-Hasan and his historic indiscretion at his own wedding?

HARUN AL-RASHID:
No.

[*Wedding music begins.*]

CLARINETIST:
Know then, my lord, that there was once a great merchant, Abu al-Hasan, a man of exquisite refinement, of perfect and complete manners, who, in his middle years, decided it was time to take a wife. And so—

[*A* WOMAN *sings the following as the* MEN *perform a little dance, led by* ABU AL-HASAN, *who is very vain and serious. The* BRIDE *is brought in by the* WOMEN.]

WOMAN [*singing*]:
Rise up and sing the season, Abu al-Hasan is getting married.
A rich merchant, and a gentleman, see how perfectly his form is
    carried.

So dignified and somber, with elegance beyond comparing;
His steps could teach a ship to sail, his glances warm the very air.

[*All the* WOMEN *join in, singing.*]

And, as they say, a glad wife is like a golden almanac
Whose rose-scented leaves are delicately pointing back

[*The* WOMAN *sings alone.*]

To the wedding season, where the breeze of benediction carries;
So rise up, sing the season, Abu al-Hasan is getting married.

[*Music continues.*]

CLARINETIST:
The lovely young wife took her seventh and last tour of the room,
Abu al-Hasan came forward with a slow and dignified step into the
chamber, and to prove that he was a man of gravity and good manners he went to receive the wishes of the old women. But at that
moment [*music ends*], with a belly full of heavy meat and drink, he
did something that he did not mean to do, may Allah preserve us all
from doing the same!

[*The* CLARINETIST *bends over behind the bowing* ABU AL-HASAN *and
produces a large fart noise. When he runs out of breath, he is followed by at least two more performers doing the same. In the middle of this, the* WOMEN *shake their jewelry to try to cover the noise
and say the following lines.*]

WOMEN:
I think it's just—just marvelous how—just how—just how marvelous all this—all this wedding—is.

[*They fall silent. The fart continues. Finally, it ends. Long pause.*]

ABU AL-HASAN:
Excuse me.

[*He tiptoes away; with each step comes a little fart. The* WOMEN
*strike up percussive instruments and begin the following chant.
The various travels of* ABU AL-HASAN *are illustrated by the company of* MEN.]

WOMEN:
Oh what an enormous fart!
Shouldn't have eaten those chickpeas.

Al-Hasan you better fly far
Shouldn't have eaten those chickpeas.

Fly on out of here, al-Hasan,
Get out of town as fast as you can,

Get on a horse while you can,
Shouldn't have eaten those chickpeas.

Ride to the coast, al-Hasan.
Oh what an enormous fart.

Dive in the sea as best you can.
Oh what an enormous fart!

How could you be so indiscreet?
Shouldn't have eaten those chickpeas.

Pistachio nuts and almond cream—
Now you've got to swim to sea.

Get on a boat and row row row;
Shouldn't have eaten those chickpeas.

Sail as far as the Malabar Coast.
Shouldn't have eaten those chickpeas.

Load up a camel, join a train;
Go through the desert with a caravan.

Oh what an enormous fart!
How will you ever live it down?

Go over mountains, find a town,
And live there for ten years.

[*The* WOMEN *now become* ABU AL-HASAN'S FRIENDS *in India. One of them plays a little tune on a zither.*]

FRIEND OF ABU AL-HASAN:
Al-Hasan, why do you look so sad?

ABU AL-HASAN:
I have lived here, in India, for ten years. I've been happy, prospered. But I long for my native homeland. For, as the poet says,

ABU AL-HASAN AND FRIENDS:
Ah, the Ganges
Ah, the Ganges
Silver river men put first;
How can an Egyptian sate his native Egyptian thirst
Save in the smile of the mild Nile?
Save in the smile of the mild Nile?

ABU AL-HASAN:

I can resist the solicitations of my soul no longer. I must return home!

CLARINETIST:

With that, the noble Abu al-Hasan packed his bags and traveled home, over treacherous mountains filled with lions, snakes, and ghouls. Until at last he reached a hill that overlooked his native land. His heart swelled at the sight.

ABU AL-HASAN:

Ah, how beautiful is my native land! No doubt I am assumed dead and long forgotten. I shall travel the streets in disguise, lest my poor old father see me unexpectedly and the shock prove too much for him.

[*He passes by a* MOTHER *and her* CHILDREN.]

FIRST CHILD:

Mother, what day was I born?

MOTHER:

Why, you were born on the twelfth day of Ramadan.

SECOND CHILD:

And what day was I born?

MOTHER:

Why, you were born two weeks after the great sandstorm.

THIRD CHILD:

And, Mother, what day was I born?

MOTHER:
Why, you were born in the year, and on the day, that Abu al-Hasan let his fart.

ABU AL-HASAN:
My fart has become a date on the calendar? It shall live as long as there are palm trees!

CLARINETIST:
With that he turned and fled, and he did not cease his flight until he was back in India, where he lived in the bitterness of exile until his death.

CHORUS:
Allah pity him!

[*The triangle is struck.* SHAHRYAR, SCHEHEREZADE, *and* DUNYAZADE *come into center stage rolling with laughter. They imitate the fart noise, by themselves and on each other. The* WAZIR *comes forward with the shroud, hears the laughter, and departs, puzzled. Then they stop.* SHAHRYAR *raises his knife to* SCHEHEREZADE, *but then he kisses her. While they kiss,* SCHEHEREZADE *takes the knife from him and passes it to* DUNYAZADE, *who then waves the audience away and covers her eyes.*]

DUNYAZADE [*whispering*]:
Intermission. Intermission.

ACT II

[MUSICIANS *are playing. The company enters. The music stops, and the finger cymbals ring once.*]

CHORUS:
But when the five hundred and first night had come . . .

DUNYAZADE:
Sister, why do you not start at once with the anecdotes you promised us concerning that delightful poet, Abu Nuwas, the khalifah's friend?

SHAHRYAR:
Scheherezade, it would give me great pleasure to hear one or two of those adventures, for I'm sure they are most entertaining; but tonight my mind is more inclined to higher things and would rather hear words of wisdom from you. If you know some tale which can fortify our souls with moral precepts and help us to profit by the ex-

perience of the wise, begin at once. Afterward, we may hear some
other sort of story.

SCHEHEREZADE:
By chance I have been thinking all day of a story which concerns a
girl called Sympathy the Learned.

[DUNYAZADE *groans.*]

And I'm ready to tell you all that I have heard of what she did and
what she knew.

SHAHRYAR:
Begin at once.

[*The finger cymbals ring once.* HARUN AL-RASHID *is surrounded by
his* COURTIERS *and* SAGES.]

SCHEHEREZADE:
One day, as Harun al-Rashid was sitting in judgment and feeling
more than the usual weariness of his soul—

FIRST SAGE:
My lord, there is a young woman and young man at our door who
beg an audience.

HARUN AL-RASHID:
Who are they?

FIRST SAGE:
My lord, the girl claims to be more learned than any man on earth.
She wishes to challenge the masters of art and science of our king-

dom to a contest of knowledge. She says that she will claim the coat of honor of each sage over whom she is victorious, but if she is defeated by a single question she will agree to be your slave.

HARUN AL-RASHID:
Send her in at once. Now all you theologians, doctors, and poets, you may examine the learning of this girl in all directions. Spare no pains in exhibiting your own scholarship and erudition.

[SYMPATHY THE LEARNED *enters. She is followed closely by a* YOUNG MAN *who holds a parasol over her head.*]

What is your name?

SYMPATHY THE LEARNED:
I am called Sympathy the Learned.

HARUN AL-RASHID:
Tell me, Sympathy, in which of the various branches of knowledge do you excel?

SYMPATHY THE LEARNED:
My master, I have studied syntax, poetry, civil and canon law, music, astronomy, geometry, arithmetic, the law concerning inheritance, and the art of reading ancient inscriptions. I know the Sublime Book by heart. I am acquainted with architecture, logic, and philosophy; with eloquence, language, rhetoric, and the rules of versification. I have carried my education so far that only those who have worn out their life in study may see it, as it were, upon the far horizon. Tell me, which of you is the most learned in the Koran and the traditions of our Prophet (upon whom be prayer and peace)?

FIRST SAGE:
I am that man.

SYMPATHY THE LEARNED:
Then let us begin. Ask me what you will of your own subject.

FIRST SAGE:
Who is your lord?

SYMPATHY THE LEARNED:
My lord is Allah.

FIRST SAGE:
Who is your Prophet?

SYMPATHY THE LEARNED:
Muhammad (upon whom be prayer and peace) is my Prophet.

FIRST SAGE:
What is your orientation?

SYMPATHY THE LEARNED:
Mecca.

FIRST SAGE:
Who are your brothers?

SYMPATHY THE LEARNED:
All Believers are my brothers.

FIRST SAGE:
Since you know the Book of Allah, can you give me an example of
your study?

SYMPATHY THE LEARNED:

The Koran is composed of 114 chapters, 70 of which were dictated at Mecca and 44 at Medinah. It is divided into 621 divisions called decades and into 6,236 verses. It contains 79,439 words and 323,670 letters, to each of which attach 10 special virtues. The names of 25 prophets are mentioned: Adam, Noah, Ishmael, Isaac, Jacob, Joseph, Elisha, Jonah, Lot, Salih, Hud, Shuaib, David, Solomon, Dhul-kafl, Idris, Elias, Yahah, Zacharias, Job, Moses, Aaron, Abraham, Jesus, and Muhammad—upon all of these be prayer and peace! And 9 birds or winged beasts are mentioned: the gnat, the bee, the fly, the hoopoe, the crow, the grasshopper, the ant, the bulbul, and the bird of Jesus (upon whom be prayer and peace!), which is none other than the bat.

FIRST SAGE:

Very precise. Tell me, how do you know that there is a God?

SYMPATHY THE LEARNED:

By reason.

FIRST SAGE:

And where is the seat of reason?

SYMPATHY THE LEARNED:

In the heart, from whence inspiration rises to the brain.

FIRST SAGE:

What is the aim of prayer?

SYMPATHY THE LEARNED:

To lift my soul toward the calm places.

FIRST SAGE:
Ya Allah! That is an excellent reply. What is the value of prayer?

SYMPATHY THE LEARNED:
It sustains faith.

FIRST SAGE:
What is the utility of prayer?

SYMPATHY THE LEARNED:
True prayer has no terrestrial use whatsoever, but it lightens the
heart.

FIRST SAGE:
An admirable reply. What is the meaning of the words "to fast"?

SYMPATHY THE LEARNED:
To abstain.

FIRST SAGE:
What is the meaning of the words "to give"?

SYMPATHY THE LEARNED:
To enrich oneself.

FIRST SAGE:
"To go on pilgrimage"?

SYMPATHY THE LEARNED:
To attain the end.

FIRST SAGE:
"To make war"?

SYMPATHY THE LEARNED:
To defend oneself.

FIRST SAGE:
Speak to me of Holy War.

SYMPATHY THE LEARNED:
A Holy War is that undertaken against the Infidels when Islam is in danger. It may only be fought for defensive purposes, never offensive.

FIRST SAGE:
What is the principal aim of life?

SYMPATHY THE LEARNED:
To cultivate enthusiasm.

FIRST SAGE:
In truth I am short of questions and arguments. This girl astonishes me with her knowledge and clarity.

SYMPATHY THE LEARNED:
I would like, in my turn, to ask you one question: if you cannot answer, it will be my right to take away the distinctive garment which you wear as a learned reader of the Book.

FIRST SAGE [*with a condescending laugh*]:
I accept.

SYMPATHY THE LEARNED:
What are the seventeen branches of Islam?

FIRST SAGE [*uncertainly*]:
Seventeen?

SCHEHEREZADE:
The First Sage reflected. For an hour.

HARUN AL-RASHID:
If you can give us the answer, the robe belongs to you.

SYMPATHY THE LEARNED:
They are: observance of the Book's teaching, conformation with the traditions of the Prophet, avoidance of injustice, to eat permitted food, never to eat unpermitted food, repentance, study of religion, to do good to enemies, to be modest, to comfort the servants of Allah, to pardon when one is strong, to be patient in misfortune, to know Allah, to know his Prophet (upon whom be prayer and peace!), to resist the suggestions of the Evil One, to fight against wicked instincts of the soul, to be wholly vowed in confidence to the service of Allah.

FIRST SAGE:
I am vanquished.

[*He hands his robe to her; she gives it to the* YOUNG MAN *behind her. The* FIRST SAGE *scurries away, as do a couple of other* SAGES.]

SYMPATHY THE LEARNED:
Who is next?

SECOND SAGE:
You have spoken of things of the spirit. Let us turn to things of the body and the world. What do you think of fruit?

SYMPATHY THE LEARNED:
It is the healthiest of foods.

SECOND SAGE:
Give an exact account of copulation.

SYMPATHY THE LEARNED [*turning to* HARUN AL-RASHID]:
My lord, I am able to answer this honorable doctor, but the honorable doctor is attempting to shame me into silence.

HARUN AL-RASHID:
Speak freely. No one will laugh at you.

SYMPATHY THE LEARNED:
Copulation is that act which unites the sexes of man and woman. It is an excellent thing, having many virtues and conferring many benefits: it lightens the body and relieves the soul, it cures melancholy, tempers the heat of passion, attracts love, contents the heart, consoles in absence, and cures insomnia.

SECOND SAGE:
What thing lives always in prison and dies when it breathes the free air? Also, what are the best fruits?

SYMPATHY THE LEARNED:
The first is a fish, and the second, citrons and pomegranates.

SECOND SAGE:
What breathes and yet is lifeless?

SYMPATHY THE LEARNED:
The morning. For in the Book it says, "The morning breathes as . . ."

SECOND SAGE:
Yes, thank you. Solve the following problem if you can: A flock of

pigeons alighted upon a tree, some upon the upper branches and some upon the lower; those upon the upper branches said to those upon the lower, "If one of you flies up to us our number will be double yours; if one of us flies down to you, our numbers will be equal." You may take your ti—

SYMPATHY THE LEARNED:
There were twelve pigeons in all, seven upon the upper branches and five upon the lower. If one of the lower flew up to the higher, there would be eight above, which would be the double of four; but if one of the higher flew down to the lower, there would be six in each position. But Allah is all knowing.

SECOND SAGE [*very frustrated*]:
Do you think we will have rain this month?

SYMPATHY THE LEARNED:
Commander of the Faithful, I will not speak unless I have your permission to reveal all my thoughts.

HARUN AL-RASHID:
It is permitted.

SYMPATHY THE LEARNED:
Then I ask you lend me your sword for a moment so I may cut off the head of this astronomer who is an agnostic and an unbeliever! I must teach you that there are four things which only Allah knows: the hour of our death, the sex of a child in its mother's womb, what will happen tomorrow, and whether or not it's going to rain.

SECOND SAGE:
My question was asked to test you.

SYMPATHY THE LEARNED:
Now let me ask my question. What are the three classes of stars?

SECOND SAGE:
Three classes—of stars?

SYMPATHY THE LEARNED:
The stars are divided into three classes: some are fixed like torches in the celestial vault that they may light the earth; others are invisibly suspended in the air that they may illuminate the sea; and the third class of stars moves at will between the fingers of Allah—we see them passing through the air at night. Give me your robe.

[*He does. She hands it to the* YOUNG MAN *behind her. The* SECOND SAGE *departs along with one or two others. More continue to sneak away throughout her tests.*]

THIRD SAGE:
Young lady, I am the most learned man of our century and I am ready to hear you declare yourself vanquished and that it is unnecessary to question you further.

SYMPATHY THE LEARNED:
And I advise you to send for garments other than those which you have on, for in a few minutes I will have taken these from you.

THIRD SAGE:
That remains to be seen. Answer this riddle: When I drink, eloquence issues from my lips; I walk and I speak in silence; I am never honored in my lifetime, and after my death I am not regretted.

SYMPATHY THE LEARNED:
A pen.

THIRD SAGE:
I am a bird, and yet I have neither flesh, blood, feathers, nor down; it is hard to say whether I am alive or dead; my color is silver and gold.

SYMPATHY THE LEARNED:
You have taken far too many words to signify a simple egg. Ask me something more difficult.

THIRD SAGE:
Exactly how many words did Allah say to Moses?

SYMPATHY THE LEARNED:
One thousand five hundred fifteen.

THIRD SAGE:
What is the origin of creation?

SYMPATHY THE LEARNED:
Allah made Adam from mud, mud from foam, foam from the sea, sea from the darkness, darkness from light, light from a fish, the fish from a ruby, the ruby from a rock, the rock from water, and the water he made by saying, "Let it be!"

THIRD SAGE:
There are two friends who have never enjoyed each other though they lie every night in each other's arms: they are guardians of the house and only separate in the morning.

SYMPATHY THE LEARNED:
The two leaves of a door.

THIRD SAGE:
By Allah, that is an admirable reply!

SYMPATHY THE LEARNED:
Now answer me, Master of Riddles. She is slim, tender, and of a delicate taste; she is as straight as a lance but has not a lance's sharpness. Her sweetness is useful on an evening in Ramadan.

THIRD SAGE [to HARUN AL-RASHID]:
My lord, it is well known that no woman is permitted during—

SYMPATHY THE LEARNED:
Give me your robe!

THIRD SAGE:
My lord!

SYMPATHY THE LEARNED:
Sugarcane is the answer. Give me your robe.

[He does. She gives it to the YOUNG MAN. SYMPATHY THE LEARNED, the YOUNG MAN, and HARUN AL-RASHID are now alone.]

HARUN AL-RASHID:
May I examine you?

SYMPATHY THE LEARNED:
I would be delighted.

HARUN AL-RASHID:
What is sweeter than honey?

SYMPATHY THE LEARNED:
The love of children.

HARUN AL-RASHID:
What is sharper than a sword?

SYMPATHY THE LEARNED:
The tongue.

HARUN AL-RASHID:
What is the joy of a moment?

SYMPATHY THE LEARNED:
The joy of love.

HARUN AL-RASHID:
What is the joy of a week?

SYMPATHY THE LEARNED:
The joy of marriage.

HARUN AL-RASHID:
What is the debt which even the wicked cannot escape paying?

SYMPATHY THE LEARNED:
Death.

HARUN AL-RASHID:
What is the desolation of life?

SYMPATHY THE LEARNED:
Poverty.

HARUN AL-RASHID:
What is the most precious thing after health?

SYMPATHY THE LEARNED:
Friendship.

HARUN AL-RASHID:
What is the strength of the heart?

SYMPATHY THE LEARNED:
Joy.

HARUN AL-RASHID:
What is the strength of the mind?

SYMPATHY THE LEARNED:
Truth.

HARUN AL-RASHID:
What is the strength of the body?

SYMPATHY THE LEARNED:
Submission.

HARUN AL-RASHID:
What is desire?

SYMPATHY THE LEARNED:
Poison.

HARUN AL-RASHID:
Charm?

SYMPATHY THE LEARNED:
An empty room.

HARUN AL-RASHID:
Madness?

SYMPATHY THE LEARNED:
A road we have forgotten.

HARUN AL-RASHID:
What comes to all of us in the end?

SYMPATHY THE LEARNED:
Happiness.

HARUN AL-RASHID:
What makes kings?

SYMPATHY THE LEARNED:
Words.

HARUN AL-RASHID:
What makes the world?

SYMPATHY THE LEARNED:
Words.

HARUN AL-RASHID:
What can destroy an empire?

SYMPATHY THE LEARNED:
Words.

HARUN AL-RASHID:
Will you marry me and be my queen?

SYMPATHY THE LEARNED:
No.

HARUN AL-RASHID [*after a pause*]:
I could compel you.

SYMPATHY THE LEARNED:
I know.

HARUN AL-RASHID:
I will give you five hundred thousand—

SYMPATHY THE LEARNED [*kneeling*]:
My lord, I am a freeborn woman of noble birth. I have not always lived like this. This boy you see holding my parasol is my brother. When my father died he left us with an abundant fortune, but my brother squandered our inheritance. He has no brains at all, and no use but to shade me from the sun. Yet as Allah lives, I love him; because my hidden heart is foolish, and I will not leave him.

HARUN AL-RASHID:
My child, I have a hundred slaves to hold your parasol—

SYMPATHY THE LEARNED:
Then keep them. And leave my brother his only task; for if you deprive him of it, he may die of shame. I beg you to deny us your great offer, and let us go our way.

HARUN AL-RASHID:
My child—

SYMPATHY THE LEARNED [*standing*]:
Kings do not need Sympathy. She must lie with those less fortunate.

[SYMPATHY THE LEARNED *and her* BROTHER *depart. The triangle chimes. The* WAZIR *steps forward with the shroud.* DUNYAZADE *has fallen asleep.*]

SHAHRYAR:
That Sympathy was a clever girl. And yet I think you are more clever still, for you have remembered all she said, and more. Tell me, what did she mean there, at the end?

SCHEHEREZADE:
I might be able to explain, my lord, but I see my father is standing at the door with my shroud.

SHAHRYAR:
He can wait another day, I think.

SCHEHEREZADE:
May I not speak to him?

SHAHRYAR:
No.

[*Pause.*]

SCHEHEREZADE:
How is your heart tonight, my lord? Is it covered or uncovered?

SHAHRYAR:
Uncovered, I think.

SCHEHEREZADE:
Could you bear a sad tale then?

SHAHRYAR:
Yes. Provided it is well stuffed with poems.

SCHEHEREZADE:
Then listen, and I will tell you of the night Harun al-Rashid met himself upon the water.

SHAHRYAR:
Met himself?

[*The finger cymbals ring once. This story, particularly the* AZIZ *and* AZIZAH *section, should be almost entirely underscored with music.*]

SCHEHEREZADE:
One night, when that great, wise king was dark within his heart, he said to his wazir,

HARUN AL-RASHID:
Jafar, I have a desire to walk the quiet night streets of Baghdad as far as the Tigris.

JAFAR:
I will accompany you as always, my lord, along with Masrur your sword-bearer. Shall we disguise ourselves as merchants once again?

SCHEHEREZADE:

The three left the palace by the secret door and walked in disguise through the quiet streets of Baghdad—City of Peace and Poets, upon which be eternal blessing. Sometimes in that dark night they believed they had lost their way, but at last they came to the river-bank of the gentle Tigris.

[HARUN AL-RASHID, JAFAR, AND MASRUR *approach an* OLD BOATMAN.]

HARUN AL-RASHID:

Old man, we would be very much obliged to you if you would take us on board your little boat and row us about for a while on the river to enjoy the delicacy of the night breeze. Here is a dinar for your trouble.

OLD BOATMAN:

What are you asking, gentlemen? Don't you know the order? Don't you hear the bell of the khalifah's boat coming toward us even now?

HARUN AL-RASHID:

Old man, that boat cannot possibly contain the khalifah himself.

OLD BOATMAN:

As Allah lives, is there anyone in Baghdad who cannot recognize the khalifah, our own Harun al-Rashid, with his wazir Jafar and Masrur his sword-bearer?

HARUN AL-RASHID:

We are strangers to this fair city and do not know the khalifah. Take us out on the river that we may see him.

OLD BOATMAN:

Are you mad? He has issued an order forbidding anyone, great or small, young or old, noble or simple, to be upon the river. Whoever disregards this order shall have his head cut off.

JAFAR:

Here are two dinars. Put us in your little boat and row under one of the sunken arches of the bridge. We must see this khalifah.

OLD BOATMAN:

I can't resist your gold, good sir. Climb aboard. Be silent.

HARUN AL-RASHID [*aside, to* JAFAR]:

I have not been on the river in a year, Jafar, and never have I issued any such an order.

OLD BOATMAN:

Hurry, I hear his music even now.

[*The boat of the khalifah comes fully into view; the* MOCK KHALIFAH (AZIZ), *played by the same performer who plays* SHAHRYAR, *is dressed as* HARUN AL-RASHID *and is standing at the helm. The company on the boat sings something simple, such as the phrase "on the gentle Tigris," mournfully.*]

There they are, the great khalifah, Jafar, and the noble Masrur.

[*They watch the passing of the boat with its singing occupants.*]

HARUN AL-RASHID:

Old man, are you sure the khalifah goes out in his illuminated boat like this every night?

OLD BOATMAN:
Indeed, good sir, he has done so for the past year.

HARUN AL-RASHID:
We are strangers on our travels, with a strong taste for interesting and beautiful things. Here are ten dinars. Row us in the track of that boat. You need not be afraid. We are in darkness, and they are in bright light. I want to see this beautiful illumination as long as possible.

SCHEHEREZADE:
They followed the mock khalifah along the river until they came to a park which sloped down to the shore. The mock khalifah disembarked with his company. The old man hid his boat in the gloom, and the khalifah's company disembarked as well. But they had only gone twenty paces when they were recognized as intruders.

MOCK KHALIFAH (AZIZ):
Who are you? How and why have you come here?

HARUN AL-RASHID:
We are strangers to this country. We only reached Baghdad today and, walking at random, came to this place without knowing this garden was forbidden.

MOCK KHALIFAH (AZIZ):
Since you are strangers, you need have no fear. Had it been otherwise you would certainly have had your heads cut off. Come with us now and be our guests for the evening.

SCHEHEREZADE:
They entered a magnificent hall carpeted with yellow silk, where the strange khalifah seated himself upon a golden throne.

MOCK KHALIFAH (AZIZ):
Ah, how weary I am after spending the whole day in doing judgment, receiving wazirs, chamberlains, amirs, and lieutenants, and forwarding the affairs of state. Let us have some music.

[*A* WOMAN *steps forward.*]

WOMAN [*singing*]:
I am drunk with love
But the cup is held to my lips
And I must drink again.
Why should I not wander in these ways
Forgetting food?
There is no joy in all these roads;
For I cannot meet my beloved
Or one who has known my beloved
Or one who has known one
Who has known my beloved.

[*As she sings, the* MOCK KHALIFAH (AZIZ) *slowly tears his robe and cries. He exposes the skin on his back.*]

HARUN AL-RASHID [*aside, to* JAFAR]:
As Allah lives, did you see his back? It is a pity that so noble a man should bear the scars of whips—a certain sign that he is an escaped criminal.

MOCK KHALIFAH (AZIZ):
Why this air of astonishment and these whispers?

JAFAR:
My friend was just saying that he has journeyed over many lands

and seen the fashion of their kings without finding any as generous as our host. He also expressed his astonishment at seeing you tear a robe which must have been worth at least ten thousand dinars.

MOCK KHALIFAH (AZIZ):
You shall have ten thousand dinars for that compliment, and a robe such as this as well.

HARUN AL-RASHID [to JAFAR]:
Ask him the cause of his scars.

JAFAR [to HARUN AL-RASHID]:
It would be better to be patient—

HARUN AL-RASHID [to JAFAR]:
Ask him now!

MOCK KHALIFAH (AZIZ):
What is this great secret of yours?

JAFAR:
Nothing but good.

MOCK KHALIFAH (AZIZ):
Tell me what you are saying.

JAFAR:
My friend noticed that your back has been cut about with rods and whips—a sign which greatly astonished him. He was anxious to know what terrible adventure has caused our master the khalifah to receive such a punishment.

MOCK KHALIFAH (AZIZ):
Clear the room.

[*Everyone leaves except the* MOCK KHALIFAH (AZIZ), HARUN AL-RASHID, JAFAR, *AND* MASRUR.]

Since you are strangers, I will tell you what you want to know. But you must carry my secret to the grave. Swear to me.

[*They swear.*]

My lords, I am not Harun al-Rashid, khalifah of Baghdad, but simply Aziz, son of the chief of Baghdad jewelers. I have money enough to sustain all this, yet it is nothing but shadow.

[*A young girl,* AZIZAH, *approaches and lies down with him.*]

I had an orphan cousin named Azizah, whose father when he died requested that someday she marry me. My parents had us always together, so that we became inseparable. We slept together in the same bed all our lives in innocence: yet, looking back, I think Azizah knew more than I about such things, for sometimes she pressed her thighs to mine, and sometimes she lay upon my back in the morning, and once she kissed me—here.

[AZIZAH *kisses his cheek.*]

On the day of our wedding I was returning from the bath, fresh scented and ready, when I remembered a friend I had forgotten to invite, and so I began to walk quickly to his house, but I lost my way.

CHORUS:
Ah, how hot it is.

AZIZ:
I sat down to rest,

CHORUS:
Ah, how hot it is.

AZIZ:
and then . . .

[*Music. The* OTHER WOMAN *walks past* AZIZ, *dropping a handkerchief deliberately and then making signs to* AZIZ *with her hands. He picks up the handkerchief.*]

That little handkerchief was enough to cover up my whole life. I was insane with love for the unknown.

CHORUS:
Ah, how cool the night breeze is.

AZIZ:
I waited for her return.

CHORUS:
The stars came out.

AZIZ:
I waited for her return.

[*He does not move. The music ends.*]

AZIZAH:

Aziz, you missed our wedding, and your father is furious. He forbids us to marry for another year. All our guests, the amirs and merchants and the kadi, waited for a long time, but then they left. Why have you behaved in this way?

AZIZ:

I am in love.

AZIZAH:

Oh?

AZIZ:

I am in love with the unknown.

AZIZAH:

What has happened?

AZIZ:

I told her the whole story, including all the signs the woman gave to me which I did not understand.

AZIZAH:

My lucky cousin, this lady loves you just as surely as you love her. The signs she gave you mean she has a passion for you and promises a meeting in two days.

AZIZ:

You see, gentlemen, my cousin loved me so that she devoted herself to helping my pursuit. And she was right in every way.

[*Music. The* OTHER WOMAN *enters and repeats her actions.*]

I met the unknown woman again and again, and each time she would not speak, but gave me signs incomprehensible to me, but clear to Azizah. A mirror placed in a bag . . .

AZIZAH:
The setting sun.

AZIZ:
A ball . . .

AZIZAH:
She fears your heart is idle in the air.

AZIZ:
A lantern extinguished . . .

AZIZAH:
The need to be discreet.

AZIZ:
Some lotus beans . . .

AZIZAH:
From the Tree of Job, Father of Patience; she reminds you this virtue is necessary for lovers.

[*The music ends.* AZIZ *lies down with his head in* AZIZAH's *lap.*]

AZIZ:
Oh, Azizah, my heart is breaking. How much longer must I wait?

AZIZAH:
Lovers often have to suffer and endure through years and years of

waiting. You have hardly had to wait a month. Perfume yourself with musk for her.

[*Music begins.*]

AZIZ:
At last, after many trials and proofs, all communicated in signs, the unknown woman yielded to me. She led me to her house.

AZIZAH:
Never betray her, my cousin, never betray her. And remember, when you finally have her in your arms, be sure to say these lines to her:

AZIZ AND AZIZAH:
If the red beating heart could speak
You would hear it saying
That love is weak, and very weak,
And the end of love is breaking.
Though in all indiscretion there is a death,
Too much discretion can cut short the breath.
Say these lines, and say them whole,
To the other woman who destroyed my soul,
And she will understand.

[*The music ends.*]

OTHER WOMAN:
As Allah lives, she who said these lines to you is now dead. I trust that she was no relation of yours, for I tell you she is dead.

[*The triangle chimes evenly as if to mark the hours.*]

AZIZ:

She is my betrothed, the daughter of my uncle.

OTHER WOMAN:

What are you saying, why do you lie? It can't be true—if she were your betrothed you would have loved her!

AZIZ:

But it is true.

OTHER WOMAN:

As Allah lives, I would never have taken her man away from her if I had known! Tell me, did she know of our meetings?

AZIZ:

It was she who explained all your signs to me. I would never have won you but for her good counsel and advice.

OTHER WOMAN:

Then you have caused her death, Aziz.

AZIZ:

It isn't true!

[*He runs to his home.* AZIZ'S MOTHER *is holding the body of* AZIZAH.]

AZIZ'S MOTHER:

My son, I wish you to tell me in what way you broke Azizah's heart. Tell me how you killed her.

AZIZ:

I did not kill her. How was I to know she loved me in that way?

AZIZ'S MOTHER:
She left something for you when she died.

[*She holds up a note.*]

AZIZ:
Let me see it.

AZIZ'S MOTHER:
No, my son. She made me swear not to give it to you until you had truly grieved, and you have not truly grieved.

[*Music begins.*]

AZIZ:
I left my mother's house and returned to my beloved. Instead of mourning Azizah I forgot myself in pleasure while my beloved built a marble tomb for Azizah. All went well for a year until one day, returning from the baths, fresh scented, I saw a girl standing in a door to a garden and, from the loose strings of her drawers, it was clear to me she had been engaging in some very pleasant activity, alone.

GIRL IN THE GARDEN:
Come into my house, stranger. Come in and pass the time of day with me.

AZIZAH [*continuously, under the following, until* AZIZ's *poem*]:
Never betray her, never betray her, never betray her.

AZIZ:
My child—

GIRL IN THE GARDEN:
Don't be afraid. What harm is there?

[*Embracing her.*]

AZIZ:
She was a young girl, lifting her robe in the garden
There was no sin a lover of love could not pardon;
She was as narrow as virtue; as easy as flying.
But I was only halfway in, when her petulant sighing
Stopped me. And I asked, "Why? Why?" and she said with a laugh,

GIRL IN THE GARDEN:
Moon of my eyes, I sigh for your other half!

AZIZ [*moving away*]:
Farewell, sweet girl.

GIRL IN THE GARDEN:
Where do you think you are going? Do you think that the door of freedom is as large as the door of entrance? Undeceive yourself, silly Aziz. The door of my house opens only once a year.

AZIZ:
So I stayed there a year, living as an animal—eating, drinking, and making love. But at the end of twelve months I heard the door groaning on its hinges and I ran into the street. I came to the garden of my beloved, and there she was. I have never seen a face so sad.

[*The music ends.*]

OTHER WOMAN:
Miserable wretch! I know where you have been. Do you think I am as patient as Azizah? Do you think that I am going to pine away and die for your infidelities? Detestable Aziz! You are like a buck who is too much in heat! Slaves!

AZIZ:
Ten women set upon me, my good lords. They tied me down, and with a hot knife, they unmanned me. They threw me from the house. I ran back to the girl behind the door, but she would not have me.

GIRL IN THE GARDEN:
Aziz, you have lost all that was ever valuable in you.

[*He turns to his* MOTHER.]

AZIZ'S MOTHER:
I see now that you are truly grieved. Here is the letter of Azizah.

AZIZ:
I unfolded that old paper and began to read.

AZIZAH:
I could not say I had a secret for your ears
But my eyes said so.
I could not say that you had caused my tears
But my eyes said so.
I could not say, My fingers mean I love you;
I could not say, My brows are meant to move you;

I could not say, My heart is here to prove you;
But my eyes said so.

AZIZ:
How many times have I heard that voice since?

[*The* CHORUS OF WOMEN *repeats the poem above in a round, each one starting after the one before has said, "I could not say."*]

AZIZAH AND HALF OF THE WOMEN:
You taught my heart to burn while yours was resting
You taught my eyes to watch while your eyes slept.
Your careless head upon my breast lay nesting
And dreamed another woman while I wept.
So dig my grave deep, and set this verse above:
"She fears not death, for she has known love."

OTHER HALF OF THE WOMEN [*simultaneously with the above*]:
Why did you look away, my love, my love?
Why did you leave me all alone?

[*They repeat until the poem is finished.*]

AZIZ:
I beat myself, gentlemen, for shame. And it is such deep shame that compels me to borrow robes of majesty. For when I ride out at night upon the Tigris and I gaze at my reflection in the illuminated water, I dream I am a khalifah . . . instead of just a fool—a fool who lost Azizah. Ah, how perfect it must be, to be a khalifah. To be Harun al-Rashid. How perfect just to be someone else.

[*No one moves, but we are now in the palace of* SHAHRYAR. AZIZ *is now* SHAHRYAR. *The* WAZIR *stands with the shroud.*]

SCHEHEREZADE:
My lord, it is dawn, and my father has returned with my shroud.

[*No response.*]

My lord?

SHAHRYAR:
Tell me stories, many stories. Tell me quick.

CHORUS:
But when the [*each performer names a different number between five hundred and one thousand*] night had come, she said, "There was once in the antiquity of time and the passage of the age and of the moment"—

[*The following section contains all or parts of six stories, told simultaneously. The performers move from one story to another just in time to take on different parts in those stories and then leave the story for another when they are not needed. Thus, the two WOMEN in "Harun al-Rashid Judges of Love" might become the TWO LITTLE GIRLS in "Hard Head and Little Foot," then divide as one becomes the TORTOISE in "The Prince and the Tortoise" while the other might play one of the SISTERS-IN-LAW. SCHEHEREZADE spends the entire time saying, "But when the nine hundred and fifty-first night had come, she said," and then "But when the nine hundred and fifty-second night had come, she said," and so on, ringing the finger cymbals after each "she said." She should come right to one thousand at the end of this "Confusion of Stories." Much of the detail of the following texts will be lost. It is up to the performers and the staging to bring out what feels essential or most interesting in each story.*]

STORY 1: THE PRINCE AND THE TORTOISE

KING:

—a king who decided it was time for his three sons to marry. "My sons, good and evil chances are not to be told beforehand, and against the decree of destiny there is no provision. Therefore, I wish that each of you blindfold yourself, spin around many times, dance in all directions, and then shoot an arrow. You will marry the woman to whom your arrow falls the closest."

PRINCE:

The two elder brothers met with evident success. But the arrow of the third brother fell upon a house whose owner was not known. The prince set forth to visit the house and found in it no inhabitant but a large and lonely tortoise. "By Allah!" said the boy's father, "you must not marry such a creature. Try again." But the arrow fell again upon the house of the large and lonely tortoise. "By Allah!" said the boy's father, "you must not marry such a creature. Try again." But the arrow fell again upon the house of the large and lonely tortoise. By Allah! She is written in my destiny. I have no predilection for tortoises in general. It is this particular one whom I wish to marry.

KING:

My son, you cannot possibly be married to a tortoise!

PRINCE:

My arrow landed by her house, and by Allah, I will marry her.

KING:

What can you be thinking? To marry yourself to such a creature?

PRINCE:

I have no predilection for tortoises in general. It is this one I wish to marry.

KING:

Look, your two brothers have found themselves decent brides.

PRINCE:

This is the wife I want, for she has told me that although she is a tortoise, she is an excellent cook.

FIRST SISTER-IN-LAW:

Soon the king fell ill from chagrin that he had a tortoise for a daughter-in-law.

TORTOISE:

But the tortoise cooked a soup that cured the king.

FIRST AND SECOND SISTER-IN-LAW:

While the other two wives were helpless in that regard.

SECOND SISTER-IN-LAW:

There was a feast to celebrate the king's recovery.

FIRST AND SECOND SISTER-IN-LAW:

The two sisters-in-law decked themselves out in finery and laughed out loud at the tortoise.

PRINCE:

But then she stood up and poured soup over her head.

TORTOISE:

And when she did, the soup turned to emeralds which clattered across the floor, and she herself changed into a princess.

FIRST AND SECOND SISTER-IN-LAW:

The two sisters-in-law poured soup over their heads, but it stayed soup.

PRINCE:

Not everything is as it seems.

STORY 2: HARUN AL-RASHID JUDGES OF LOVE

[*Story 2 begins at the end of the* KING's *first line in story 1.*]

HARUN AL-RASHID:

One night, Harun al-Rashid, lying between two fair girls whom he loved equally, could not decide with whom he should finish.

HARUN'S FIRST GIRL [*to the* SECOND GIRL]:

You are keeping the capital for yourself and you will not even let me have the interest.

HARUN'S SECOND GIRL:

I have a right to the capital, according to these words of the Prophet (upon whom be prayer and peace!): He who makes the dead earth live again shall own it for himself.

HARUN'S FIRST GIRL:

The capital belongs to me, according to these words of the Prophet (on whom be prayer and peace!): Game shall belong not to him who starts it but to him who kills it.

HARUN AL-RASHID:
When the khalifah heard these quotations, he considered them so much to the point that he satisfied both the girls on that one night.

STORY 3: ALA AL-DIN ABU SHAMAT AND THE INFAMOUS PEDERAST BILATERAL

[*Story 3 begins simultaneously with story 1.*]

BILATERAL:
—an infamous pederast called Bilateral, whose favorite poem was:

Not to hear the fools who said:
"Ah you loved too fair a being,"
Not to see the shaking head
Wag, "He trusted to his seeing,"
I stopped my ears with the enchanted song:
"Though death come after,
There is no need to fear,
Life is long and made for laughter."

But then one day, he saw the fairest young man on earth.

ALA AL-DIN:
Ala al-Din Abu Shamat, who had lived his whole life, up to that moment, in the cellar of his parents' house.

BILATERAL:
I must trick this fine young man into journeying out into the desert. I will teach his friends to sing:

FRIENDS:
Sing the joys of vagabonding
All that's beautiful travels far.

A pearl must leave the ocean's bonding
And be drawn to where the merchants are:
Far across the sandy beaches
Before it shows and glows and reaches
The cream-white neck of some young girl.

ALA AL-DIN:
Ala al-Din Abu Shamat felt so ashamed that he had never traveled
that he saddled up at once and rode for the desert.

DESERT THIEVES:
Where he was immediately set upon by thieves.

BILATERAL:
Bilateral came across him in the desert, half naked. His heart grew
sick, for he felt himself to be the cause of this misfortune.

ALA AL-DIN:
I have lost everything!

BILATERAL:
Although Allah has taken your fortune, he has preserved your life:

Your gold is lost, your life is spared:
That is to say:
Your fingernails have been pared—
A thing of every day.

Come with me, I will clothe and feed you.

ALA AL-DIN:
Ala al-Din had no choice but to accept the kindness of Bilateral.

ALA AL-DIN AND BILATERAL:
And they went to supper beneath his tent.

[BILATERAL *tries to kiss* ALA AL-DIN.]

ALA AL-DIN:
As Allah lives, my kind Bilateral, I do not sell that kind of goods!
The only consolation I can give you is the assurance that if ever I
sell it to others, I will give it to you for nothing.

BILATERAL:
Dear boy, don't you know:

Lust is not content with blushes,
Kisses taken from pure lips,
Not content with wedded glances:
Lust must have a thing which dances,
Lust must have a thing which gushes,
Lust must have a thing which drips.

ALA AL-DIN:
I cannot understand why you so harp upon this one string! I can
only repeat that on the day I sell this thing, I will give it to you for
nothing.

STORY 4: A SONG FOR TWO EXPERIENCED WOMEN

[*Story 4 begins at the end of story 3.*]

TWO EXPERIENCED WOMEN [*singing*]:
Green girls think men are all alike
Because each wears a turban;

But one will be a country tyke
And one a knowing Urban,

One will be a white and shining star
One murky, lacking culture;
One a clean feed, as eagles are,
And one a corpse-fed vulture.

STORY 5: PRINCESS BUDUR

[Story 5 begins simultaneously with story 1.]

TWO GENIES:
—two genies flying through the air, arguing.

FIRST GENIE:
I tell you, Cousin, you have never seen a prince so fair as the one
I've just left behind, Prince Kamar al-Zaman—

SECOND GENIE:
And I tell you, Cousin, that if you were to see my princess, even in a
dream, you would fall into an epilepsy and bubble like a camel!

FIRST GENIE:
The first genie then saw the sleeping Princess Budur and agreed it
would be best to transport her to the sleeping prince.

*[The sleeping PRINCESS BUDUR is transported to the sleeping KAMAR
AL-ZAMAN. During the following, they individually wake and fall
back to sleep, speaking to each other.]*

SLEEPERS:
Sleeper, the palm trees drink the breathless noon,
A golden bee sucks at a fainting rose,
Your lips smile in their sleep. Oh, do not move.

Sleeper, oh, do not move the gilded gauze
Which lies about your gold, or you will scare
The sun's gold fire leaping from your hair
As dark as the separation of friends.

Sleeper, oh, do not move; your breasts in sleep,
Allah, they dip and fall like waves at sea;
Your breasts are snow, I breathe them like sea foam,
I taste them like white salt. They dip and fall.

Sleeper, they dip and fall. The smiling stream
Stifles its laugh, the gold bee on the leaf
Dies of much love and rosy drunkenness,
My eyes burn the red grapes upon your breast.

Sleeper, oh, let them burn, let my heart flower,
Fed on the rose and santal of your flesh,
Burst like a poppy in this solitude.
In this cool silence.

STORY 6: HARD HEAD AND LITTLE FOOT

[*Story 6 begins after the* TWO GENIES' *exchange in story 5.*]

HARD HEAD:
—a boy who was born with a hard head and willful temperament . . .

LITTLE FOOT:
And a girl with a tender soul and delicious little feet.

MOTHER:
Children, I am your mother and I am about to die. Little Foot, I require you to swear that you will never go counter to your brother's will, no matter what.

LITTLE FOOT:
I swear.

[MOTHER *dies.*]

HARD HEAD:
Listen, I am going to put every single thing which we own—furniture, cows, buffalo, goats, money, everything—into the house and set fire to it.

LITTLE FOOT:
But if you do that, dear brother, what will become of us?

HARD HEAD:
I just want to.

LITTLE FOOT:
But—

HARD HEAD:
And further, I would like to set fire to some of the neighbors' houses as well.

LITTLE FOOT:
What will become of us?

HARD HEAD AND LITTLE FOOT:
The wild-eyed owners of the other houses armed themselves with pitchforks and ran after the two children to kill them.

LITTLE FOOT:
Save me! Save me!

[*They run away to a farm.*]

O Brother, let us behave ourselves here and offer to work on the farm, and be friendly with the owner's three children.

HARD HEAD [*to* TWO LITTLE GIRLS]:
Let's go out to the threshing floor and play at flails. I'll go first.

TWO LITTLE GIRLS:
We'll beat you as though you were grain.

[*They do. Everyone is delighted.*]

HARD HEAD:
Now it's my turn.

[*He beats them so hard they scream and die.*]

LITTLE FOOT:
Brother! What have you done? You've impasted these children into the floor! We must fly! We must fly, my brother! And we were doing so well on the farm!

[*They run away and climb a tree.*]

Thank goodness we've found refuge in a tree—now be very quiet, my brother, for the farmers are below us.

HARD HEAD:
I'm going to do things on their heads.

LITTLE FOOT:
Oh, don't do it, dear. They don't know we're up here.

HARD HEAD:
I want to.

FARMERS:
Cut down that tree!

LITTLE FOOT:
Now we will surely die!

GENIE:
Just then, a genie passing by flew down and carried them up on his arms.

LITTLE FOOT:
At last we're safe!

HARD HEAD:
I'm going to tickle this genie's belly.

LITTLE FOOT:
Brother, don't!

HARD HEAD:
I want to!

[*He tickles the* GENIE, *who laughs and drops them.*]

LITTLE FOOT:
Brother, look, you have landed on some ghoul and killed it. What shall we do? Oh, here comes the king! Hide behind a rock.

KING:
Little daughter of benediction, did you kill this ghoul?

LITTLE FOOT:
My brother did, O King, but I swear it was an accident!

KING:
And where is the fine fellow?

LITTLE FOOT:
You will not hurt him.

KING:
Most certainly not!

LITTLE FOOT:
Then here he is.

KING:
O chief and crown of bravery, I thank you for killing this ghoul who has kept my kingdom dark for years. I give you the hand of my only daughter in marriage, and because of her delicious little feet, I take your sister to be my queen.

HARD HEAD:
It is permitted!

[*As the performers each finish their individual stories, they join with* SCHEHEREZADE *in counting off the nights. When they all get to the one thousandth night they stop; we hear the last two lines of the* SLEEPERS' *poem above. Silence.*]

SHAHRYAR:
Scheherezade, marvelous girl, you have lifted the veil from my heart.

SCHEHEREZADE:
My king—

SHAHRYAR:
You must never leave me now, you must stay here by me always and whisper in my ear, only to me. You are safe here now, I swear—

SCHEHEREZADE:
I know the hour is late, O auspicious king, but I have one more story, just one more very subtle tale to tell. Let it be one thousand nights and one night before you grow weary of me—

SHAHRYAR:
I shall never grow weary of—

SCHEHEREZADE:
Then listen to the tale of "The Forgotten Melody." It has come down to us through the writings of Ishak of Mosul, the great musician of our time, that—

[*She rings the finger cymbals once.*]

122

SCHEHEREZADE AND ISHAK OF MOSUL:
One night

ISHAK OF MOSUL:
I went to visit Harun al-Rashid and met a stranger there, a sheikh from al-Hijaz.

HARUN AL-RASHID [*to* ISHAK]:
Honorable musician, you will be pleased to know this man, for he is al-Fadl, the grandson of Maabad of al-Hijaz.

ISHAK OF MOSUL:
A benediction! Prayer and peace upon the grandson of the most accomplished musician of our age.

HARUN AL-RASHID:
Perhaps if you are agreeable to him, he will sing one of his grandfather's songs, for he has a fine memory and a charming voice.

ISHAK OF MOSUL:
Most noble Sheikh al-Fadl, tell me, if you will, how many songs your grandfather composed.

SHEIKH AL-FADL:
Only sixty.

ISHAK OF MOSUL:
Would it be trespassing too far upon your patience if I begged you to name your favorite?

SHEIKH AL-FADL:
Easily the finest of them all is the forty-third.

ISHAK OF MOSUL:
Without hesitation, he picked up his lute and began to sing. And as he sang, the walls of the room moved closer in to listen.

[*The room is silent. We do not hear the music.*]

And time was frozen in my blood, and I left the prison of my skin and became other than myself. How can I describe . . . how can I . . . how . . . ?

[*He is lost in the silence.*]

SHEIKH AL-FADL:
Would you like to play it over with me, or shall I have it transcribed? I leave for Medinah tomorrow, and I doubt I shall pass this way again.

ISHAK OF MOSUL:
No, no. I will remember that, I will remember it all my life. Thank you, thank you, Sheikh al-Fadl, and your noble grandfather Maabad, blessed among musicians.

I hurried home and stuffed carpets and pillows in the windows and by the door. This ancient song, which no one else has heard, shall now be mine! And I shall keep it for myself and play it only for myself in solitude.

I took down my lute and tuned it to perfection. But as Allah lives, I could not play that air which had moved me so.

[*The* CHORUS *begins very quietly to chant "What, what, what, what is it?" The chant gradually grows louder and more urgent under* ISHAK OF MOSUL's *entire speech.*]

I could not remember one note of it, could not even call to mind the mode in which it had been written. I can usually retain a hundred couplets and their melody when I have listened once and with a negligent ear, but this time it was as if an impenetrable woolen curtain had fallen between the music and my mind.

Night and day I racked my brains and spurred them to remember, but it was useless. At last, in despair, I left my lute and my singing lessons and all my students behind and I went journeying throughout Baghdad, through Mosul and Basrah, and finally through the whole of Iraq questioning the oldest singers concerning Maabad's forty-third song. But none of them knew it or could help me to it.

Rather than be ridden eternally by this obsession, I made up my mind to cross the desert to far Medinah to find the sheikh himself and beg him to sing the song again. I was in Basrah, riding by the river, when I came to this decision. Suddenly three young women appeared from nowhere.

[*The chanting ends. Three* WOMEN *approach. One of them takes hold of the bridle of* ISHAK's *donkey.*]

WOMEN BY THE RIVER:
A benediction, a benediction, traveler!

ISHAK OF MOSUL:
Let go, let go!

FIRST WOMAN BY THE RIVER:
Will you not answer us?

ISHAK OF MOSUL:
Oh, please, just let me go.

FIRST WOMAN BY THE RIVER:

Where is your passion for Maabad's forty-third song, O Ishak? Have you given up your search? We were behind the curtain of the harem, Ishak. We watched you when that old man sang his song. Ishak, I thought you had gone mad.

ISHAK OF MOSUL:

I am madder now than ever, looking for that song! For pity's sake let me go on!

FIRST WOMAN BY THE RIVER:

If I can sing you that song, will you still go to Medinah?

ISHAK OF MOSUL:

Don't torture me!

FIRST WOMAN BY THE RIVER:

By Allah, I know that song and I may teach it to you.

ISHAK OF MOSUL [*dismounting and kneeling*]:

I would give anything to hear it, even if it were sung off the key, even if it were cut. I would give ten years of my life to recover one note of that song.

FIRST WOMAN BY THE RIVER:

Ah, Ishak, we know your character. We know the greed with which you hoard your own compositions. No pupil has ever learned more than one song from your own lips or been allowed to sing more than one song which you have made yourself.

ISHAK OF MOSUL:

But my songs are my greatest possess—

FIRST WOMAN BY THE RIVER:
Ishak, how can you think that it is you who sings or plays, or that it is al-Fadl of Medinah, or even Maabad of al-Hijaz? It is not you, nor they, nor I. Don't you know that it is God?

ISHAK OF MOSUL:
Mistress—

FIRST WOMAN BY THE RIVER:
How could you have forgotten that it is God, Ishak? You must swear to me that if I teach you the forty-third, you will willingly sing it and every other song you know to whomever you may meet upon the road.

ISHAK OF MOSUL:
Mistress, I swear. And if I meet no one on the road, from now on I will sing to the insects and to the stones and to the sky itself.

ISHAK OF MOSUL AND SCHEHEREZADE:
And she said,

FIRST WOMAN BY THE RIVER AND SCHEHEREZADE:
Then listen . . .

ISHAK OF MOSUL:
and she began that song at half voice in my ear, and her two companions began to dance, and the vault of heaven came closer in to listen, and the stars began to dance, and the river and all its life began to dance.

[*In silence, the two* COMPANIONS *begin a dance made up of the ordi-*

nary gestures of everyday life—perhaps tying a shoe, spreading a cloth, etc. Slowly, and at first clumsily, SHAHRYAR *joins them.*]

SHAHRYAR [*quietly searching*]:
What, what, what, what is it?

[SHAHRYAR *suddenly "hears" the silent music and begins to dance as the others do, a simple dance of the everyday, familiar and mysterious at the same time.* SCHEHEREZADE *joins him; one by one the entire company joins in. Then it is over. The* WAZIR *stands with the shroud.*]

SHAHRYAR:
Scheherezade, it is dawn, and your father has come with your shroud.

SCHEHEREZADE:
My king?

SHAHRYAR:
How can that poor old man have lived so long in a silent house? How he must have suffered, and how frightened he must have been—for your sake—all this time . . .

SCHEHEREZADE:
My king—

SHAHRYAR:
You and Dunyazade must return home now to comfort him in his old age. The door is open, Scheherezade, my bride. You must go now.

SCHEHEREZADE:
But, my lord, what should my father think of me, were I to abandon my little children?

SHAHRYAR:
What do you mean? What children?

HARUN AL-RASHID:
He took her up and sat her by his side.

WOMAN BY THE RIVER:
She sent Dunyazade from the room.

JESTER:
But before she could explain,

DUNYAZADE:
Dunyazade returned.

ABU AL-HASAN:
She had with her three small children:

SHAHRYAR:
a boy, one year old,

PERFECT LOVE AND THE GIRL IN THE GARDEN:
and infant twin girls,

SYMPATHY THE LEARNED:
born during the long days of Sympathy the Learned

MADMAN:
and hidden from the king.

SHAHRYAR:
What is there not to love?

CHORUS:
Everyone rejoiced.

ISHAK OF MOSUL:
Scheherezade's father, the wazir, was sent for

WAZIR:
and told to put away her shroud.

DUNYAZADE:
And Dunyazade was married

ROBBER:
to the king's brother, Shazaman.

PASTRYCOOK:
And they lived year after year in all delight,

HARUN AL-RASHID:
knowing days each more admirable than the last.

ALL:
And the nights over Baghdad were whiter than the days.

[One or two company members produce the sound of air-raid si-
rens and of static on a distant radio and the rising of the wind.]

And the nights over Baghdad were white . . .
And the nights over Baghdad were whi . . .

[*The company looks up, then sinks to the ground. The sound of the wind rises, and everyone begins to roll away, first slowly, then all at once, like dead leaves in the wind. Some performers pile on top of one another against the back wall of the theater; others are strewn about, caught on the ottomans or the instruments. The sound of the wind continues for a moment, then stops. Everyone is still.*]

IMPROVISATION IN
"THE WONDERFUL BAG"

"The Wonderful Bag" (see page 64) may be improvised within the framework of the following lines by different actors selected by chance during each performance. As they enumerate the contents of the bag, the Kurd and the Persian are free to say anything to expand their lists, adding detail or wandering off the point. They may be as outrageous as they like, but they should try to avoid naming objects that are too modern or making references that are too local.
Here are the framework lines:

GREENGROCER:
One day, in the marketplace of Baghdad, someone let fall a little bag and walked on without noticing.

[*He throws the bag in the air; there is a battle for it. Whichever performer gets the bag first takes the role of the* PERSIAN, *and whoever speaks up first after that will be the* KURD.]

KURD:
What are you doing, trying to walk off with this bag as though it belonged to you ever since you were born?

PERSIAN:
O Mussulmen, save my goods from this wretched unbeliever who wishes to make off with my bag!

KURD:

My bag is known and well known. It is universally acknowledged to be my bag!

[*The* KADI *enters.*]

KADI:

Hold on here! Who is the plaintiff and who the defendant?

[*He takes the bag from the* PERSIAN.]

PERSIAN:

Allah increase the power of our kadi and judge! This bag is my bag. I lost it and found it again in the street today!

KADI:

When did you lose it?

PERSIAN:

I lost it yesterday, and I could not sleep all night for thinking of it.

KURD:

May Allah lift up and honor our master the kadi. I lost that bag two weeks ago and have not slept for thinking of it since.

KADI:

The truth can be uncovered soon enough! Whoever is the true owner of the bag shall best be able to describe its contents. Each of you give a list, and whoever's list is closest to a true inventory of the contents shall own the bag and everything in it.

KURD:
O Kadi,

[*The performer here gives an initial, medium-length list, starting with possible objects, such as "a candlestick, a lemon," and proceeding to considerably larger, perhaps more improbable objects. Whatever the performer chooses to say, the final words will be:*]

and all are ready to swear that this bag is my bag.

PERSIAN:
Kadi, let me say that in this bag

[*The* PERSIAN *gives his or her first list, then ends with:*]

all ready to bear witness that this bag is my bag.

KURD:
I ought to add that, in this bag, besides the things I've mentioned, there are

[*The* KURD *gives a longer description, one which may involve many detours and explanations, ending with:*]

all ready to swear that this bag is my bag.

PERSIAN:
As I now remember, O Kadi, there is, in the bag, in addition to what I mentioned before

[*The* PERSIAN *gives a longer description, which ends with:*]

all ready to protest to the kadi if the kadi does not recognize my rights and say that this bag is my bag!

KADI:
As Allah lives, either you are two rascals mocking at the law and its representatives, or this bag is a bottomless abyss or the Valley of the Day of Judgment itself. Let us see what is in the bag.

[*He empties it onto the floor.*]

A little orange rind and some olive stones.

PERSIAN AND KURD:
All right, it's yours.

[*At this point, the dialogue returns to the script.*]

My recommendation for production is to improvise the story. Without doubt, a few cast members will excel at this, while others will not; some will never even want to try. On certain nights the scene will soar, and on others it may be excruciating: slow, awkward, not very funny. But the attempt itself is always exciting; it creates a situation wherein the performers become like Scheherezade herself and must entertain an audience alone and under pressure.

Below is the only record of any "Wonderful Bag" improvisation. It was captured when the show was taped for radio broadcast. It is neither the best nor the worst "Bag," and it is a little too long, but I include it to give an idea of what might happen on any given night. The performers in this case were Larry DiStasi as the Kurd and David Kersnar as the Persian. They did not stick precisely to the lines of the framework.

KURD:

Very wise Kadi, and may I say that that is a very, very nice hat you're wearing this afternoon. The contents of the bag . . . within that bag, Kadi, there are some black beans, there is a large piece of lint that I was forming into a swan—I do lint sculpture—there is also, um, within that bag a butterfly who had some honey stuck to his wings. He was having trouble flying and I . . . I picked him up and did him the favor of putting him in the bag with the lint sculpture and I'm sure they are playing together a little bit. There is also, within that bag, a very sick cat, Kadi; he has hoof-and-mouth disease—which is very odd for a cat, Kadi, but he was hanging around with some horses which are also within that bag and they are all ready and willing to swear that that bag is my bag.

PERSIAN:

Preposterous. May I name the contents of that bag and we'll get on with this? There is within that bag, uh, a few quills. There is within that bag a little canister of ink. There is within that bag some parchment. There is within that bag—I'm a writer, you see—there is within that bag—you probably sagaciously sagaged [sic] that, uh, there is also within that bag—not a very good writer—there is within that bag is [sic] my ghost writer—within that bag—who, uh, I hire on alternate Tuesdays to just kind of clean up my work, here's uh, I , uh, was, was, actually, it was . . . had lost it two Tuesdays ago, you see it's Tuesday and I've not gone on with my work and, you know, deadlines and everything. Anyway, it's my bag. It's, it's my bag. It's . . . my bag. It's my bag.

KURD:

Kadi, this man is clearly unstable. There are a few items which I forgot to mention which are also within that bag, my bag. There is, within that bag, a large golden cow, Kadi, and inside of the belly of that large golden cow there are many, many jewels, Kadi, and . . . and gold and silver and when you squeeze on the udders they all come out, Kadi. It's really quite wonderful, and I would be willing to share any quantity of these jewels with you because the cow just keeps producing, it's really fantastic, Kadi. There is also within that bag a very small, small pyramid which I can balance on my nose, a very entertaining trick. There is also the River Nile, the cities of Baghdad and Basrah, there is also a very large, large condor, Kadi, who is circling around Baghdad; it is very ominous and frightening in there, and there are people down below, and they're . . . they're screaming, Kadi, they are very upset about this condor, Kadi, because he has very sharp teeth—I don't know if you've ever seen a condor with very sharp teeth, Kadi, but they can be pretty frightening. And . . . well, he's circling around and there is also a tidal wave forming, right near Baghdad, I don't know if you can picture this, but there . . . there's this tidal wave forming and there are jumping flying fish also with very large teeth, Kadi, and the people are screaming and there's a volcano that's growing up out of the ground, Kadi, and it . . . it's just very upsetting to me . . .

[*Here he begins to cry.*]

and all these people are ready and willing to swear that that bag is my bag.

PERSIAN:
If I may mention a few other things which I forgot that are within the bag. There is also within the bag—there are some butterflies. There are some—a few—ants, red and black. They all are depictions of my next work that I'll be writing. They come from . . . it's . . . it's about a butterfly farm that's being attacked by some army ants and they are trying to carry off all of the ants; in fact, they're flying off

with them. And it's . . . as . . . as I say, it needs tightening up and that's why I need my ghost . . . sage, rather scribe—

[*Here, one of the other performers shouted out, "Good premise, though!"*]

Good. Thank you, thank you. But, I do, do need that scribe, because what's incredible is that within, been with me for thirty, forty years, and he's been able to take on my exact likeness. You know, my best features, my long flowing hair, and my upstanding, um, form, of, um, my body. And what's actually incredible there's also within that bag enough rope to hang myself. There's within that bag—well, anyway, they are all willing to swear, and I'll give you a few butter-flies and a couple of ants—we'll throw it in—it's my bag, it's my bag, it's . . . my . . . bag.

Good luck.

A NOTE ON THE CASTING

The stories in the play are as follows:

ACT I
Opening
The Madman's Tale
The Perfidy of Wives
    The Dream (The Pastrycook's Tale)
    The Contest of Generosity (The Butcher's Tale)
    The Wonderful Bag (The Greengrocer's Tale)
    Abu al-Hasan's Historic Indiscretion (The Clarinetist's Tale)

ACT II
Sympathy the Learned
The Mock Khalifah
    Aziz and Azizah
The Confusion of Stories
    The Prince and the Tortoise
    Harun al-Rashid Judges of Love
    Ala al-Din Abu Shamat and the Infamous Pederast Bilateral
    A Song for Two Experienced Women
    Princess Budur
    Hard Head and Little Foot
The Forgotten Melody
Closing

The original division of roles among sixteen performers was as follows. Where necessary for clarity, the character name is followed by the story name in parentheses.

FIRST WOMAN: Scheherezade; Aziz's Mother

SECOND WOMAN: Dunyazade; Dancing Girl and Fool ("The Madman's Tale"); Jester's Wife; Azizah; Little Foot and Second Genie ("The Confusion of Stories")

THIRD WOMAN: Perfect Love; Other Woman ("Aziz and Azizah"); Harun's First Girl, Tortoise, and Little Girl ("The Confusion of Stories"); Woman by the River ("The Forgotten Melody")

FOURTH WOMAN: Slave Girl ("The Madman's Tale"); Girl ("The Contest of Generosity"); Girl in the Garden ("Aziz and Azizah"); Sleeper ("The Confusion of Stories"); Woman by the River ("The Forgotten Melody")

FIFTH WOMAN: Dancing Girl and Fool ("The Madman's Tale"); Butcher ("The Perfidy of Wives"); Bride ("Abu al-Hasan's Historic Indiscretion"); Singer ("The Mock Khalifah"); Mother, Experienced Woman, and First Sister-in-Law ("The Confusion of Stories"); First Woman by the River ("The Forgotten Melody")

SIXTH WOMAN: Dancing Girl ("The Madman's Tale"); Woman ("Abu al-Hasan's Historic Indiscretion"); Sympathy the Learned; Harun's Second Girl, Experienced Woman, Little Girl, and Second Sister-in-Law ("The Confusion of Stories")

FIRST MAN: Shahryar; Mock Khalifah/Aziz

SECOND MAN: Harun al-Rashid; Sheikh al-Islam ("The Madman's Tale"); both Kings ("The Confusion of Stories")

THIRD MAN: Wazir (to Shahryar); Fool ("The Madman's Tale"); Clarinetist ("The Perfidy of Wives"); Old Boatman ("The Mock Khalifah"); Friend, Desert Thief, and Farmer ("The Confusion of Stories")

FOURTH MAN: Camel (opening); Figure and Fool ("The Madman's Tale"); Greengrocer and Robber ("The Contest of Generosity"); Kadi ("The Wonderful Bag"); Friend, Desert Thief, Farmer, and Genie ("The Confusion of Stories"); Donkey ("The Forgotten Melody")

FIFTH MAN: Principal Musician; Prince of Fools ("The Madman's Tale"); Jester; Sympathy's Brother; Hard Head and First Genie ("The Confusion of Stories")

SIXTH MAN: Principal Musician; Jafar; Fool ("The Madman's Tale"); Pastrycook; Farmer, Friend, and Desert Thief ("The Confusion of Stories"); Sheikh al-Fadl ("The Forgotten Melody")

SEVENTH MAN: Fool ("The Madman's Tale"); Sheikh ("The Contest of Generosity"); Third Sage ("Sympathy the Learned"); Bilateral ("The Confusion of Stories"); Ishak of Mosul ("The Forgotten Melody")

EIGHTH MAN: Shop Assistant ("The Madman's Tale"); Poor Man ("The Dream"); Boy ("The Contest of Generosity"); Ala al-din abu Shamat ("The Confusion of Stories")

NINTH MAN: Chief of Keys; Man in the Dream ("The Dream"); Abu al-Hasan; First Sage ("Sympathy the Learned"); Masrur ("The Mock Khalifah"); and Prince ("The Confusion of Stories")

TENTH MAN: Camel (opening); Madman; Chief of Police ("The Dream"); Second Sage ("Sympathy the Learned"); Sleeper ("The Confusion of Stories")

COPYRIGHT © GERRY GOODSTEIN (MANHATTAN THEATRE CLUB)

Shahryar (Christopher Donahue) and Scheherezade (Jenny Bacon)

COPYRIGHT © GERRY GOODSTEIN (MANHATTAN THEATRE CLUB)

The Madman (Bruce Norris), Perfect Love (Ellen Bethea), and the shop assistant (Jesse L. Martin)

COPYRIGHT © CYNDI FINKLE (LOOKINGGLASS THEATRE COMPANY, ACTORS' GANG)

Perfect Love (Jane Cho) and her entourage

Musicians (from left: Joey Slotnik, Doug Hara, Temple Williams, and Mark Brodie)

COPYRIGHT © CYNDI FINKLE (LOOKINGGLASS THEATRE COMPANY, ACTORS' GANG)

The greengrocer (Joey Slotnik), the clarinetist (David Kersnar), and the pastrycook (Temple Williams)

COPYRIGHT © GERRY GOODSTEIN (MANHATTAN THEATRE CLUB)

The kadi (Ramon Melindez Moses)

COPYRIGHT © GERRY GOODSTEIN (MANHATTAN THEATRE CLUB)

The wedding party of Abu al-Hasan (from left: Ramon Melindez Moses, Faran Tahir, Bruce Norris, Denis O'Hare, Jesse L. Martin, and Enrico Colantoni)

COPYRIGHT © GERRY GOODSTEIN (MANHATTAN THEATRE CLUB)

Abu al-Hasan (Jesse L. Martin)

The mock khalifah (Adam Dannheiser) with his attendants

COPYRIGHT © LIZ LAUREN (LOOKINGGLASS THEATRE COMPANY)

Aziz (Christopher Donahue)

COPYRIGHT © GERRY GOODSTEIN (MANHATTAN THEATRE CLUB)

The wazir (David Kersnar) with Scheherezade's shroud

COPYRIGHT © LIZ LAUREN (LOOKINGLASS THEATRE COMPANY)

ABOUT THE PLAYWRIGHT

Mary Zimmerman's credits as an adapter and a director include *Metamorphoses*, *The Odyssey*, *Journey to the West*, *Eleven Rooms of Proust*, and *The Notebooks of Leonardo da Vinci*. Her work has been produced at the Lookingglass Theatre and Goodman Theatre of Chicago; on Broadway at Circle in the Square; in New York at Second Stage, the Brooklyn Academy of Music, and the Manhattan Theatre Club; at the Mark Taper Forum in Los Angeles; and at the McCarter, Berkeley Repertory, and Seattle Repertory theaters as well as many others around the country and abroad. The recipient of a Tony Award for directing for *Metamorphoses* and a MacArthur Fellowship, she is a professor of performance studies at Northwestern University.